Triple Blessing

A FATHER'S STORY OF
INFERTILITY, HOPE AND LOVE

MICHAEL CAVE

Copyright © 2019 by Michael Cave

All rights reserved. This book or any portion thereof may not be reproduced or used in any manner whatsoever without the express written permission of the publisher, except for the use of brief quotations in a book review.

ISBN 978-1-7331742-0-6 (Paperback)
ISBN 978-1-7331742-2-0 (Kindle eBook)
ISBN 978-1-7331742-1-3 (ePub)

Cover design & book design by Noah Adam Paperman

To my wife, Angelique, and my children Michaela, Emma and Christopher, my inspiration for writing this book.

To my dear and longtime friend since I was 18 years old, Leslie Franklin, who was a tremendous source of support both before and after our children were born.

To my very good friend Cheryl McLagan, who has been a wonderful friend to me and my family every step of the way. Cheryl, God bless you!

Table of Contents

Foreword	i
Introduction	1
Saving All My Sperm	5
Our Story	7
What *Not* to Say to Someone Struggling with Infertility	19
Trying to Conceive—Just How Difficult It Is	29
The Social Aspect of a Pregnancy Journey	35
The Word "Journey", and Why Some Hate It	41
Angelique's Pregnancy	47
Triggers	63
"Just Adopt."	71
Words of Wisdom	79
A Passage of Deep Reflection	87
The Helpless Husband	97
The Number of Embryos to Transfer—A Difficult Decision	123
The Financial Toll	127
Dear Dad	139
Dear Mom	149
Dear Angelique	153
Dear Triplets	159

Foreword

I was twenty years old, working for an insurance company, and was also working on my master's degree in accounting when a simple ad in a newspaper completely changed my life.

I didn't know it then. After all, the plan was to get my CPA license and the idea of children was not yet in the picture. Ten years later, I am now thirty years old, and that simple "Become an Egg Donor" newspaper ad helped create the amazing four-year-old triplets known as the Cave Triplets, or "The Cavelets."

Not only did that ad put me on the path to be their egg donor, but it changed my career, brought awareness to me and my husband's own concerns with conceiving, and brought about other egg donor cycles, which helped other couples in need start their own families.

After completing my first donor cycle at age twenty-one, I knew right away that I was in the wrong profession. After several weeks of research, sending out résumés, and interviewing, I landed an Egg Donor Coordinator position as a contractor. My job was to manage egg donor cases from start to finish.

Fast forward a few donor cycles and a few years working as a coordinator, and I joined forces with an amazing colleague at another agency as a part-owner and Egg Donor Program Director.

It was in this new role that I also met Angelique and Michael Cave. My relationship with Angelique began as a way for me to share my experiences as an egg donor, to mentally and physically prepare her for her own egg retrieval. But after attempts using Angelique's own eggs failed, the Cave family and I were later reconnected again as a suggestion for them to use an egg donor and for me to actually be their donor.

I had now been married for two years, and some light was shed on me and my husband's own efforts trying to conceive (TTC). We worked out our agreement that would reduce the Caves' expenses and allow my husband and I, along with the Cave family to split the eggs retrieved.

After the egg retrieval procedure, the Caves had eleven eggs, we had ten. Our IVF cycle results weren't great: three embryos of poor quality were available to transfer by Day five of the embryo development process. For us, only one embryo successfully implanted, but unfortunately resulted in a miscarriage.

Angelique's IVF cycle had a different outcome, and she went on to give birth to triplets. I was so happy and excited for them. My job as a donor was done! But how ironic that I was a donor who was able to help so many other families find success with donor eggs, but now my husband and I are having trouble conceiving?

After that IVF round and subsequent miscarriage, three intrauterine insemination (IUI) attempts later, we had our daughter in July 2015. I did a gestational surrogacy cycle following that, for another couple, successfully delivering that child in April 2017, and then went on to have our son in November 2018.

I am thirty years old, and my egg donor days are long over. Given the complications from my last pregnancy, so is gestational surrogacy. I am not sure if we will have more children of our own either, but I look back on my twenties and still can't believe that one simple ad changed my career, put me on the egg donor path, helped to create the triplets, brought me into surrogacy, assisted me and my husband's own fertility path, and created an open and one-of-a-kind relationship with the Cave family.

Infertility is hard! Every second of this "process" to become a parent is exhausting. I only personally witnessed a small portion of what Angelique and Michael went through. I also only had a small struggle with TTC compared to so many others. For the most part, I have always been on the "other side." Angelique and Michael share a unique experience on their very long road to becoming parents. It is a reminder that every journey is different, there is no textbook way to make this work, and that we can simply find comfort in understanding another perspective.

Kayla Reveal

Introduction

Sometimes in life, we are dealt a bad hand. It's debatable why this happens, but one certainty is that it happens to everyone, and often for no rhyme or reason, as adversity is just a part of life: bad things happen, and they can really hurt and take your breath away. Infertility is an unfortunate barrier that, for some, stands in the way of a very personal decision that a human being makes for what might seem to be instinctive reasons: the decision to bring a child into the world. A child is many things, but at its most fundamental definition, a child is the product of a union between sperm and egg.

When a man and/or woman are unable to have children when trying to do so, frustration and disappointment take on a whole new meaning. When months turn to years, and something that should be fun (baby-making!) turns into work, we may question our purpose in life. Modern medicine and generous hearts have given "infertile" couples new hope and a chance to realize their dreams of having a family of their own. However, these opportunities are not free of twists, turns and unique challenges that must be overcome in order to find success.

But then sometimes your luck improves, and your fortunes are abundant. You make new connections that will change your life forever. Many things start to go right, and you find yourself anticipating success rather than failure. Old feelings of disappointment and despair are replaced with those of anticipation, excitement and joy. Rather than feeling lost at sea, you can see land on the horizon, and can't wait to set your feet on it. And when you've finally achieved that which had been so far out of reach, you realize how much more you appreciate what you now have than most people, because you know all that it took to make it happen in the first place.

I do not wish on anyone the mental, physical, emotional and financial grind that comes with the infertility journey. It changes you. Each loss takes a little (or a lot) of you. I want those struggling with infertility to know that they are not alone, and that there are many people out there who truly get it. It's not a dirty secret—it's something that happens and is a challenge for couples to try and overcome. It taxes a marriage, a couple's faith and causes you to question why it happened to you. It's a journey marked with hurtful and condescending remarks from "outsiders", feelings of jealousy, envy, impatience, guilt, anger and resentment, and, let's not forget, hope, hopelessness and despair. I personally didn't know how important having a family was to me until I was faced with the prospect of not having a family at all. I was used to succeeding, not failing. The journey is wrought with personal choices such as surrogacy, egg and/or sperm donation, adoption, selective reduction (pregnancy termination), the number of embryos to transfer, whether or not to destroy frozen embryos or keep them in long-term storage, and (go figure) whether or not to let others in

INTRODUCTION

on your struggles and journey.

You are about to read a touching story involving a couple's struggles with infertility. It has been written from the perspective of the husband in the equation, with unique insights into the world of infertility. If you are a reader who has struggled with infertility in the past, it's my hope that this book strikes a chord with you. If you are currently struggling with infertility and have not yet found success, just know that you are not alone and that there are more people who have been there before than you may realize. There are many paths to having a family, none of which are easy. I hope you enjoy reading about this particular journey, as it wasn't conventional by any stretch of the imagination. And it's not over yet: in fact, it's just beginning.

Saving All My Sperm

Written by Michael Cave

A few million swimmers
is all that we need,
We have entertainment,
videos, magazines,
Mr. X - here's your cup,
Could you please...fill 'er up?
"Sure, just give me a minute or two...
I've been saving all my sperm for you!"

My cup runneth over,
What's a guy to do?
Seal off the deposit,
and grab a tissue,
Wash my hands...and my face,
it's the end...of the race,
I've completed what they asked me to do
I was saving all my sperm for you!

Now it's time to let the sperm hounds know I'm done!
Ring the bell...and they'll come,
Oh my goodness, that was fun!
Everybody knew what I came in here to do...
I was saving all my sperm...
That's right, saving all my sperm...
I was saving all my sperm for you....for you!

Our Story

I met my wife Angelique in 2001, about a month after moving to Sacramento, California. One of the things that really stuck out about Angelique was how nurturing she was. At the time, she owned three cats: Blue (an orange male tabby and her first cat), Cleo (a black female cat with long, fine hair), and Nubay Cita (a pudgy gray female cat with white paws). Blue and Cleo were very close and usually hung out together, and Nubay Cita was always on the outside looking in and had to work harder to get her time with Angelique. Angelique caring for her cats was when I first noticed just how much love she had to give—they were her children. Somehow Angelique was able to divide her attention and love evenly between the three cats. The competition for her affection and attention was fierce, but she managed it and I really admired her for that. Deep down I knew that she would make an outstanding mother when she had kids. She was very attentive to their needs and knew how to love each cat, whether it was a snuggle in bed, a back scratch, a belly rub or scratching underneath their chin.

We dated for nearly five years before getting married on August 12, 2006. When we moved around to new locations, so did the cats—Angelique and her cats were a packaged deal. In a way, the cats were a part of her identity. It wasn't that she was a crazy cat lady or anything like that, but to me it represented just how strong her desire to love and provide for others was. Anyone with animals knows how special the bond with a pet can be, and I really didn't understand it until I met Angelique and saw how she was with her cats; she would do anything for them.

After we got married in 2006, we started losing the cats, one by one. Nubay Cita was the first to leave us after a brief battle with cancer. Angelique took the loss hard. I remember that we both ended up taking the day off work to grieve, but when it was time to put Nubay Cita down, Angelique couldn't attend, so her mother had to take her to the vet to have her put down peacefully. This was also her first major loss and experience dealing with the feelings that come with the stages of grief. About a year later, Cleo was the next to leave us due to kidney failure, followed by Blue several months after that, also due to kidney failure. Angelique was devastated and for the next few years a void existed. This is when her desire to have a child became the most apparent.

Ultimately, my wife Angelique and I had five unsuccessful in vitro fertilization (IVF) cycles (three fresh and two frozen) before deciding it was in our best interest to pursue the egg donor path to help us realize our dream of having a family. How it all came together is nothing short of remarkable and should be attributed to perfect timing and fate. It all happened so fast, considering how long it typically takes to find an egg donor. Usually, a couple is "matched" with an egg donor through an egg donor agency. In our case, Kayla, our donor, was the Egg Donor Program Director for Gestational Surrogate Moms (GSMoms), the surrogate agency we had discovered and used during the summer of 2013 when Angelique's sister had volunteered to be a surrogate for us.

Lisa, the Director of GSMoms, was someone who we reached out to in order to learn more about surrogacy. Lisa was an amazing resource with deep connections into the infertility industry. Over the course of our engagement with her, she made us aware of Dr. Bradford Kolb from Huntington Reproductive Center Fertility (HRC) in Pasadena, California. Dr. Kolb is internationally known for his expertise in complex reproductive matters and is one of the largest providers of egg donation and surrogacy in the United States, with patients travelling from around the world to HRC Fertility Pasadena to see him. His practice is also known for helping to develop and implement cutting-edge technologies in the genetic screening of embryos, the development of new laboratory technologies, and the development of highly efficient treatment. He also has very high success rates, and Angelique and I had the pleasure of meeting him and experiencing his warm bedside manner, compassion, and dedication.

That summer, Lisa put us in touch with Kayla because Angelique had been frustrated with her first IVF cycle and how the egg retrieval procedure left her in a lot of pain and essentially miserable because she suffered from ovarian hyper-stimulation syndrome (OHSS). Kayla was a pro at egg retrieval, having worn the hat of egg donor for seven previous couples, so she was asked to contact Angelique and give her some tips on how to prepare for the retrieval and how to recover afterwards. Once she called, Angelique and I were impressed with how nice and helpful she was. We had no idea at that point our paths would later cross later in a remarkable way. We ended up keeping her in the loop on our efforts in the coming months, but after the surrogate cycle failed later that summer, Angelique and I decided it was time for a change.

Lisa again recommended to us HRC Fertility in Pasadena, but we elected not to use them during the cycle that summer because we thought the travel would be too much of an inconvenience for everyone. We engaged with Dr. Kolb and proceeded to discuss the best possible options. These included 1) Thawing some or all of the remaining nine embryos being cryopreserved and transferring the best-looking ones 2) Doing another fresh IVF cycle, only with a slower stimulation protocol and Lupron trigger so that Angelique wouldn't hyper-stimulate, and finally 3) Pursuing an IVF cycle using an egg donor.

A few months prior, we had flown down to Pasadena to attend one of HRC Fertility Pasadena's free seminars. We also went for some face time with Dr. Kolb. There was a slide in Dr. Kolb's presentation that showed IVF success rates when using donor eggs, and they were consistently higher, regardless of the woman's age.

Angelique was focused on that slide the entire presentation, and noted that she was leaning towards the egg donor option. She and I talked about it after having a conversation with Dr. Kolb. We agreed that we were ready to switch doctors, as we felt that Dr. Kolb was serious about solving our case and gave us the best chance for being successful.

In our discussions with Dr. Kolb, Angelique had mentioned her concerns about how she did not adequately recover from egg retrieval cycles. Dr. Kolb mentioned that he utilized a Lupron trigger prior to egg retrieval, and that patients generally recovered from the retrieval procedure faster and avoided over-stimulating their ovaries. He also shared with us the results of his assessment of our remaining frozen embryos. They were not good quality embryos and several of them were frozen at day seven as opposed to day five, which is usually an indication that it is not a strong embryo and was unlikely to result in a viable pregnancy. Dr. Kolb went the extra mile and consulted with an embryologist after reviewing our case, and this due diligence with his research was commendable. We ended up going with option 2 (another fresh cycle with her own eggs with Dr. Kolb as our IVF doctor), and when that didn't work, we knew we were ready to pursue an egg donor.

We engaged Lisa and Kayla, informing them that we were ready to pursue an IVF cycle using an egg donor, and Kayla "dusted off" a list of potential donors she had provided us when we had been first considering it. We arrived at a short list of potential egg donors and initially chose a young woman from Montana. Unfortunately, she was booked for two cycles before we would have an opportunity to work with her, so we settled on another young woman from Twenty-Nine Palms, California. She was twenty-one years old with two kids of her own, but had never been an egg donor. Kayla scheduled a Skype conference for us to meet later that week.

A few days passed and we received an interesting call from Lisa at GSMoms. A mystery woman was now available who was a "seasoned" egg donor, having done seven previous cycles—all of which resulted in either positive pregnancy tests or live births. Lisa asked if we were interested in this person, seeing as we had already agreed to meet with another potential donor. Naturally, we said yes, so Lisa had this "mystery donor" send us her profile. When we received the profile, everything looked great. The donor, known as "Lana" was beautiful (just like my wife), with an excellent family medical history, and, best of all, proven fertility and no major red flags. We were also told that this egg donor had not cycled with Dr. Kolb before, but that Dr. Kolb had met her and knew her. The donor would be monitored locally in her state of residence and would fly out to Pasadena the week of the retrieval.

Lisa told us that when this egg donor called her that we were the first couple that she thought of as a match. We quickly informed Lisa that we wanted to secure this donor's services as soon as possible. We asked Kayla to immediately cancel the scheduled video conference with the egg donor from Twenty-Nine Palms.

Next, we arranged a video conference with the new egg donor. Lisa called me later that evening and admitted that this mystery donor was actually Kayla, the Egg Donor Program Director, and asked if this was a problem. We told her we couldn't care less and asked Lisa to lock her in. Kayla was interested in doing another egg retrieval cycle and preserving her own fertility by freezing her own eggs. To keep the cost down, she wanted to split her eggs with a couple in need: enter us.

From that point on, things moved quickly. We had the somewhat awkward (but in a good way, in that it was strange for Kayla to be the one being interviewed) GoToMeeting video conference with Kayla, facilitated by Lisa, and from there embarked on a fast-tracked IVF cycle that ultimately moved faster than anyone could have imagined.

The video conference happened the last week of February in 2014, and the legal agreement was quickly wrapped up and signed by all parties. By the second week of March, Kayla was on a plane to Pasadena for blood work. Angelique was very relieved. She was thrilled that she only had one thing to prepare her body for: receiving an embryo (who cared if it wasn't biologically hers?). She wouldn't have to again go through the physical grind of an egg retrieval. It was like a weight had been lifted off her shoulders. Kayla was very familiar with our struggles, so she was motivated to ensure that the entire process went smoothly for us.

Kayla and I proceeded to stay in touch on a regular basis—a few times a day, actually. Kayla's phone would go off at all hours of the day, and her husband, Garrett would know it was me, and it worked the same for me—both spouses just knew that they should stay out of the way and let Kayla and I "do our thing."

Both Kayla and I are very driven people with seemingly boundless energy. To avoid any perceived conflict of interest, Lisa was going to manage the cycle on Kayla's behalf, but Kayla ended up managing it herself, and that wasn't a problem because we had already established a very open relationship.

Kayla's bloodwork and other labs came back OK, but the testing done on her husband, Garrett unfortunately, revealed that there were a few issues with his sperm, so they abandoned the plan to freeze her eggs and do an IVF cycle as well. So now we had two IVF cycles going concurrently. This was Kayla's first IVF cycle and, essentially, her first taste of what we had experienced for so many years. What an unbelievably tough break—someone with great eggs and proven fertility was now discovering that her own journey to a baby would have its twists and turns. This had to have been shocking.

Soon, we all started to make travel plans. This turned out to be a nightmare to coordinate, as it was difficult to "sync up" the two women's cycles. Angelique's cycle was notoriously unpredictable, so without forcing the issue, we could have potentially been waiting a while for her period to start. In the end, we helped Angelique's period start using medication, and Kayla (by way of birth control pills) essentially ended up on standby. From there, medications were ordered for both women. Kayla was able to qualify for discounts on medications for her cycle, which saved us money in the long run and was very much appreciated.

Angelique and I had never seen a cycle go so smoothly. We kept waiting for something crazy to happen, but overall it really didn't, except for one scare. One day, towards the end of her stimulation protocol, Kayla was on a ladder in her finished basement, painting, and fell, badly spraining her ankle. Fortunately, this injury didn't compromise our IVF cycle and we were able to proceed as planned. By the time we met her in Pasadena, Kayla was hobbling, but the eggs were safe. As I reflect back on this now, it's a reminder of how one simple thing can change the course of your life forever. Had the cycle been cancelled as a result of the injury, those eggs would have been wasted, and we wouldn't have our triplets.

The egg retrieval date was scheduled for April 14, 2014, and this was the day Garrett and I had to give our semen samples that would be used in the IVF process. The embryo transfer dates for both couples were scheduled for April 19th. Angelique and I stayed at the same hotel as Kayla—the Pasadena Inn—and made arrangements to meet her for breakfast the following morning after Angelique arrived.

Kayla had a cinnamon raisin bagel, and only ate half. It was so interesting watching her sit there talking with us. She is a former beauty pageant contestant, and her posture was perfect.

I was tempted to ask her, "How would you end world hunger?", but I refrained from doing so. As the conversation went on, she relaxed a bit, and we all eventually headed over to HRC Fertility, which was right across the street, as both women had follow-up appointments. From there, we walked around downtown Pasadena, and had lunch. Then Angelique and Kayla embarked on some major girl talk about infertility and how crazy this journey had been. Angelique was due to fly back to Sacramento in a few hours (remember, Angelique wasn't doing an egg retrieval, so her work was done), so we all just sat in Kayla's room and talked. It was a great conversation, and the two women really bonded during that time. This could have gone so differently. Angelique could have chosen to have nothing to do with Kayla, which would have been her right, but given Kayla's surprising news about her husband's sperm quality requiring the couple to pursue IVF at that time, and this all being unknown territory for her (despite being in the industry), she needed a mentor/big sister, and Angelique was the perfect person to fill that role.

The egg retrieval day was wonderful. Kayla seemed calm in the waiting area (though probably nervous, as we knew she wanted a great haul of eggs for us both), and we passed the time before she was whisked away chatting about life.

After the procedure and after she was stabilized, Angelique and I were allowed to come in to visit with her. We learned that Dr. Kolb had retrieved twenty-one eggs from Kayla. Kayla repeatedly asked us if we were happy with that number, and of course we said yes. It had always been clear to us that our happiness and satisfaction were of the utmost importance to Kayla, and that she took her job seriously. Even though we were splitting the eggs with her, our contractual agreement called for us to get the odd number egg, so, of the twenty-one eggs retrieved, we were entitled to eleven. This was a much better number than the four eggs total that were retrieved with Angelique's last IVF cycle using her own eggs.

The first fertilization report came in for both Angelique and Kayla, and of the eleven eggs Angelique and I received, ten fertilized successfully for us, and ten also fertilized successfully for Garrett and Kayla. Three days later, the numbers were still neck and neck, with six of the ten fertilized eggs reaching the eight-cell stage. As we waited for Day Five to arrive, many thoughts ran through our heads. Angelique and I had done this many times before, and were fully aware that not all of the six fertilized eggs would make it to Day Five—we just hoped for one good embryo. It's nerve-wracking showing up for the Day Five embryo transfer and not knowing if you have any good embryos to transfer. You find comfort in your phone not ringing with any bad news in the days preceding or the day of the transfer. Still, we showed up to the IVF clinic, with both women's bladders extremely full, waiting and wondering for what seemed like forever. Angelique flew back to Pasadena the day before the embryo transfer procedure and stayed overnight. Garrett was not present for the embryo transfer due to work commitments. I had been in town since I arrived the day before providing my semen sample for the egg retrieval.

On Embryo Transfer Day, Kayla was whisked off first to prepare to receive her embryo(s). At that time, we didn't know how many she intended to transfer or how many she had available for transfer. We would later find out that she had three embryos of average quality and she had thrown in all three, as Dr. Kolb told her that it was likely that only one embryo would take. Angelique was called in for her embryo transfer about thirty to forty-five minutes later, and we learned that of the six that had made it to Day Three, four embryos made it to Day Five, with two being of outstanding quality, and the other two being of a quality where it could go either way. Dr. Kolb gave us suggestions of what we could do, and then left the room while we made our decision.

Our options were 1) Transfer all four embryos (with the understanding that all four could take, let alone split). 2) Transfer the best-looking two embryos and freeze the others (the other two might not make it to freezing). 3) Transfer three. We elected to transfer all four embryos we had left and let the chips fall where they may. This was understandable given all of the previous attempts.

Weeks later, both women would have blood work done (apparently Kayla started peeing on a stick during the flight back home), and we learned that both Angelique and Kayla were pregnant. Angelique's HCG (pregnancy hormone) beta numbers were very high out the gate (a strong indication of multiples), and she was understandably excited with the outcome. Her progesterone and estrogen, which were also being monitored by Dr. Kolb, were perfect as well. Follow-up beta labs revealed that the numbers were doubling every two days, as expected.

After we received the third beta results, we knew that it was at least twins, but possibly triplets or even quads. The six-week ultrasound in Pasadena confirmed that it was triplets. We weren't really in shock, as we had been preparing ourselves for the possibility of higher order multiples after we decided we were transferring all four of the remaining embryos we had.

Our decision to pursue the egg donor path was paying off. We were further along than we had ever been before in any IVF cycle, and appeared to be well on our way to becoming parents. Our last best chance appeared to be bearing fruit. We began to look forward to new milestones in a pregnancy journey that we had previously refrained from even thinking about. Angelique had feared that she could not carry a baby, yet she stared at the ultrasound monitor and saw that what was once thought impossible for her was, in fact, possible. A triple blessing, growing inside her womb: truly remarkable.

What *Not* to Say to Someone Struggling with Infertility

Generally speaking, people mean well, but when it comes to infertility, they really don't know what to say, and as a result, they end up saying the first thing that comes to mind. While it's sincere, it's usually hurtful to someone grappling with infertility. There are many other things not to say, but this list represents statements that essentially serve as triggers:

- "It'll happen when it's meant to."
- "If it's not working, it must not be meant to be for you guys."
- "Just go on vacation."
- "Just relax."
- "Why put your wife through all of that?"
- "You all need to do it in a certain position, and I *guarantee* you'll get pregnant…promise!"
- "Why don't you have kids yet?"
- "Why is it taking you guys so long?"

- "Why is having a baby so important to you?"
- "I had my babies in my early 20s…"
- "All my husband has to do is look at me and I can get pregnant."
- "Just adopt. There are tons of babies out there that could use a loving home."
- "Have you all considered adoption?"
- "If you adopt, BOOM–you'll get pregnant."
- "Just do IVF."
- "IVF is expensive…and it's not even guaranteed to work."
- "Why would you want to consider donor eggs?"
- "You already have a child of your own. Be grateful for them."

When couples hear any of these statements, it makes them not want to share their infertility issues with anyone, and it remains a secret struggle.

A person struggling with infertility has random triggers, and *anything* someone says can be perceived as insensitive and set them off. These triggers are magnified as the pregnancy losses or negative pregnancy tests mount.

As a male/husband on the other side of the equation, I can personally tell you that having an "outsider looking in" offer advice on how to overcome your infertility issues is hurtful. I certainly heard an earful from a variety of sources. My father passed away in 2008, shortly before our infertility issues consumed us, but I've always wondered what he would have said had he been alive when our struggles really took root. As badly as I know he wanted me to give him more grandchildren, he was always supportive of me. But I have always wondered what he would have thought of the challenges we ended up facing (and overcoming).

Everyone's path to a family is unique and, generally speaking, people tend to overstep their boundaries, telling couples struggling with infertility what to do. By the same token, some couples starting out in their journey have plans of what they will do, and this seems harmless—until you get into the business of trying to conceive and become consumed with it. For example, a couple might say that they will try on their own for six months, do three rounds of IVF, and if that doesn't work they will adopt.

IVF offers a higher likelihood of success than trying naturally, but it isn't a guarantee. It's also important to point out that IVF is financially out of reach for many couples. The excitement you feel in the first IVF cycle is extreme, yet so is the disappointment if it doesn't work. There are still many factors in play with IVF that impact success. They include female age, male sperm health, egg quality, uterine health, etc. Let's not forget the cost. IVF heightens the emotional aspect of trying to conceive because everything is a part of a process into which you have insights that you wouldn't have in a normal "natural cycle."

For example, you get a date on which you can do a blood pregnancy test, and, with IVF, you know exactly when fertilization took place. Most women can't resist the urge to use a home pregnancy test during their first IVF cycle, and this usually adds to the anxiety. My advice (from personal experience) is to resist the urge to do a home pregnancy test. The blood test is always more accurate, plus your wallet will thank you later. Another reason is that the blood test is used to measure the rise of the HCG pregnancy hormone in the bloodstream. Sure, a home pregnancy test can be dark from the onset or a faint line can become darker with each test, but with IVF, blood tests are the strongest indicator of pregnancy viability, although not the only indicator.

People who might say to a couple or think, "Just do IVF", last time I checked, aren't willing to write a check to a struggling couple so they can do an IVF cycle. There is very little "guessing" with IVF, as everything is tightly controlled—that's still not a guarantee, as evident by IVF's less than 100% success rate. The same "survival of the fittest" rules apply to IVF. Look at what happens after an egg retrieval. If you had twenty-four eggs retrieved, very rarely do you end up with twenty-four viable embryos to transfer.

For some women, there is a huge pride component that serves as their compass. I know my wife was put off by the high cost associated with IVF in our early years of trying to conceive, so she wanted to see if she could do it on her own. Sure, that would have been much cheaper, but that was not our reality or path.

I don't think adoption is as simple as the people recommending it as an option say it is. I was even told at one point to reconsider my position on adoption. I did, in that I became open to considering adopting three eggs from a donor once it was clear that my wife was OK with this option. We got the best possible outcome given our struggles—my wife Angelique got to carry three babies and experience pregnancy, and using an egg donor resulted in the best chances for success and was the right path for our situation.

As I went through the process of reaching acceptance with the egg donor path, I only had one condition: I wanted to know the person, and I do—very well. We couldn't have lucked out any more than we did; our donor was truly the perfect match for us.

There's also a legal aspect to adoption. Sometimes one or more of the biological parents' attempts to claim their parental right and keep the child brings on an expensive legal battle that ensues for possibly months and years. Adoption might be another path for some couples, but not for every couple.

The adoption comment upset me the most over the course of our seven and a half years of trying. My wife and I discussed this early on and didn't agree. From my perspective, it wasn't how I wanted to spend our money. It was important for me to have a biological connection to the child(ren). People seemed to try to make me feel bad for having that position, but the simple fact is that adoption isn't for everyone. While people would say that there are many kids who need a loving home that Angelique and I could provide, I think that couples that are genuinely interested in pursuing that path should seek out those children.

What we heard early on from folks that learned of our struggles was, "Just go on vacation and it will happen!" Really? An egg will release and be fertilized just because we get away? We tried that and it didn't work. When there is an underlying problem, that's simply not possible. It must work for some, but then again, these people don't tend to have a major fertility problem.

I heard the "If it's meant to be, it will be" comment a lot over the years, and each time it pissed me off. Sometimes you have to intervene and dig deep and fight for what you want. This is where modern medicine comes into play and has given many families the opportunity to realize their dreams. Things have to line up. In our case, we had to have repeated IVF failures and pursue a surrogate path in order to be exposed to new opportunities, which included a compassionate doctor and an egg donor with a high rate of successful egg donations. Now that's what I call "meant to be." But even those excellent odds didn't guarantee that it would happen.

It still took many people doing their part—the IVF doctor and his nursing staff, the egg donor, myself, and my wife Angelique.

I wouldn't fault anyone for deciding to stop treatment. IVF is emotionally exhausting and wears on you with each failure. I know personally I got increasingly frustrated with each failed attempt, and it became harder and harder to not let it show. I remember after learning from my wife about another failed attempt, I didn't even say anything. I walked upstairs into our bedroom, balled up my fists and repeatedly slammed them into the mattress. It was one of those memory foam mattresses, so it was very giving. I must have slammed my hands into that at least twenty times. I can't say that I felt better afterwards, either. Normally I am cool, calm and collected, but these failures caused me to lose my cool.

What's even worse is when women brag about how young they were when they had their kids. Were they always ready to be parents? Could they afford the child(ren)? Does that make them better than someone who had to work a little harder or who decided to have a child later in life? Absolutely not. There is definitely a fertility window of opportunity, but women don't need to be reminded of that.

The last bullet on the above list ("You already have a child of your own. Be grateful for them") actually has its rightful place among the others, in that it introduces a unique aspect of infertility called secondary infertility. In the secondary infertility scenario, the woman already has a child or children, wants to have more but, for some reason, cannot. This would seem like a pretty traumatic thing for a woman to experience because they most likely feel like their bodies, having had previous success at bearing children, have let them down.

The desire to have another child becomes magnified by the frustration and grief that come with not being able to conceive as easily as with the first child. I remember early in our fertility journey I used to read infertility blogs and this situation would be among the posts. The women felt robbed; they didn't understand why they had unexplained infertility all of a sudden, and their biological clocks started ticking even louder, which created more pressure. I will admit that when I first read these types of posts, I had the same thought—that the women should be grateful that they were able to have a child at all. That was my line of thinking before our own struggles began to drag on several years. It doesn't mean that those women love the children that they have any less—there is just a desire for more, and that's OK. For families in this situation, though, I can see how it would become an obsession of sorts, as you start to feel like you want something you can't have. And once you've "graduated" to assisted reproductive technologies like IVF and gain additional insights into the process of having babies, that pressure is magnified exponentially. Secondary infertility shows that the burden of infertility is non-discriminatory and can affect anyone, even those who have previously found success.

What's also interesting is annoying and insensitive comments don't stop after you've found success. My wife and I have heard it all, especially once folks learned we were expecting triplets, and even after we had them. People can't wrap their heads around more than one baby at a time. Here's a short list of things that I heard:

"Triplets?!? Good luck. You're going to have your hands full."

Duh? And someone else's hands will be full, too! This is the most popular comment that I have noticed. People are consumed with pointing out the obvious.

"One baby is bad enough. I can't even imagine three!"

Bad? Excuse me? Fortunately, most people, especially those who said this, don't have to imagine three. But we didn't look at it as a problem or as being bad at all —we wanted each of the three babies we have. We looked at it as our situation. This is what we were given to manage. We will get it done. Not every person can manage multiples.

"God bless you…"

Interesting tone, but thanks!

"Your life is over."

That's a particular way of looking at such a blessing. We felt that our lives could finally begin after having our children. What is wrong with people? Proof positive that some people take their responsibility as parents for granted and don't know what to say or how to say it.

"Get as much sleep as you can before they get here!" or "You're not going to get any sleep!"

Sleep cannot be banked and saved for a rainy day. It's pretty obvious that with three babies, sleep would be in short supply, as would time to do anything like we did before the babies arrived, at least for a few years.

What *Can* You Say?

You can say that you're here as a support resource. You can say "This must be exceptionally difficult", "Let me know how I can help"; "I am always here to listen if you need to talk."

It helped me to have no shortage of people who were willing to listen. Most couldn't relate, but they at least recognized that it was my struggle and saw the impact it was having on me. Some folks had no clue what my wife and I were going through because at some point I found a way to not show the pain. When you're going through this, it becomes evident how many people take their fertility for granted. It's so easy for the majority. If the amount of YouTube vlogs (video blogs) out there are any indication, it's a very common problem that people are becoming more and more comfortable talking about. The Internet has created an environment where there can be a community of support for those struggling with infertility. The flip side of the Internet is that it can also give "Internet trolls" a platform to attack posters just trying to share their story. Everyone has an opinion, and sometimes it's a very negative opinion. I've noticed that some folks on the Internet are offended that people are resorting more and more to IVF, as if it's taking the easy way out or (I've read) playing God. I've read comments from people who feel that if it couldn't happen naturally, then it was clearly not meant to be. There are now hundreds of thousands of babies worldwide that make that argument a moot point.

There are also mothers who take to the Internet to brag about how young they had their children (usually in their twenties—good for them!). They've also stated that these older (geriatric) moms are pushing the envelope and not doing the child(ren) any favors having them so late in life, because they will be really old when the child is not even eighteen. I wasn't aware that there were rules governing when people could start a family.

Trying to Conceive—Just How Difficult It Is

WARNING: Somewhat Technical

As a child, I used to believe that babies were delivered by storks in the middle of the night. Being a child was a great time to let your imagination run wild. So when I first heard the story of how babies came into the world (the stork version, not necessarily the birds and the bees version), I assumed that couples just placed an order and voilà—this perfect little bundle of joy arrived at your doorstep and you got on with your life. Finding out that this wasn't true at all wasn't nearly as disappointing as learning that Santa didn't exist. One thing my parents were good at was selling a story, with my father, William Cave, being the master of this art.

Every Christmas, when he was in town, my mom would leave eggnog and cookies by the fireplace, and he would take a bite out of one of the cookies and leave tons of crumbs on the glass plate. Every Christmas morning we'd wake to find that (and, of course, tons of presents).

Now, I'm keenly aware that babies are much harder to bring into this world. Sure, it would be nice if this tech savvy world we live in had a service where, using your iPhone or Android device, you could order a baby with an app. That would be the 21st century version of the stork approach. The fortunate couples do the baby dance and in a matter of weeks learn that they are expecting. Then there are those who weren't trying, but not actively preventing, who are surprised to find out that there's a bun in the oven. I've come to the conclusion that it's really a miracle that anyone ends up pregnant at all. It's such a short window, when you think about it. In bullet form, here's a quick run-down of what needs to happen:

- A male needs to produce plenty of good, healthy sperm that can take advantage of your peak cervical mucus conditions. Before ovulation, cervical secretions change for a woman, and this creates an environment that helps sperm travel through the cervix, uterus and fallopian tubes in order to reach the egg.
- When the egg has been fertilized, the blastocyst has to implant securely in the lining of the uterus.
- The right levels of the hormone progesterone must be produced by the corpus luteum to maintain the pregnancy.

That doesn't seem so hard, does it? Trust me, those who have struggled with infertility know that not only is it hard, but there are many factors that are entangled between these three bullets above. Allow me to list a few of the things that can cause conceiving a baby to become life's greatest challenge:

- Poor egg quality
- Low ovarian reserve

- Male factor infertility: low sperm count, poor motility and/or morphology
- Genetics: chromosomal abnormalities or other genetic mutations
- Blocked fallopian tubes
- Polycystic Ovarian Syndrome (PCOS)—infrequent or absence of ovulation
- Clotting disorders or the presence of antibodies that attack the pregnancy
- Incompetent cervix
- Uterine complications (fibroids, bicornuate or heart-shaped uterus, etc.)
- Low progesterone and/or estrogen
- Advanced maternal age (greater than age thirty-five)
- Obesity
- Unexplained (ouch!!!)

There are several other factors, but you can see that there is really no shortage of issues that can interfere with something as natural as conception. An egg actually has a very short shelf life: twenty-four hours, actually. And before it can meet up with sperm, it must first be released from an ovary as a result of a luteinizing hormone (LH) surge that is strong enough to cause this to happen. This can take up to thirty-six hours to occur. Most people who don't struggle with fertility (bless their hearts) are oblivious to the details that actually feed into what it takes to make a baby, so there's an acceptable case where ignorance is bliss.

The longer a couple struggles with conceiving a baby, the more difficult it gets to "get back on the horse." It becomes difficult to think about what the next steps should be (almost paralyzing to think about taking a step forward, actually), and even more difficult to imagine having to accept a life without a child. Unfortunately, this is the reality for many couples. It's sometimes easier to just give up—think of it as a last resort means to protect one's emotional core. Not everyone can withstand the emotional toll multiple failed IVF cycles can take on a woman's mind and body. Some even choose not to graduate to IVF. This is a very understandable choice. There are many examinations, needles, pills, hormones and other invasive procedures necessary in order to get to the point where a woman is PUPO (Pregnant Until Proven Otherwise). With IVF, you know what is happening at every step of the process, and this creates an unavoidable amount of anxiety. Hopes can be built up as high as the couple wishes, but destroyed with one phone call from the IVF clinic with bad news.

And the worry doesn't end with a confirmed positive pregnancy test. The HCG (Human Chorionic Gonadotrophin—pregnancy hormone) levels (only one of many indicators of a viable pregnancy) must continue to rise exponentially. Most IVF doctors would like the HCG levels to double every forty-eight hours. As you read other chapters in this book, you'll see that the worrying really never ends. Trying to conceive is a high-stakes game of sorts. The odds are different every month and, depending on where you are in your own infertility journey, sometimes the stakes must be raised. This is true with IVF, specifically with the number of embryos to transfer.

Coping with what's happening around you when you're trying to conceive is also extremely difficult. Everywhere you look, you usually see pregnant women, toddlers and happy families. This hasn't increased because you are struggling. It's just magnified because you want it so badly. It's very similar to buying a specific make and model of a car and suddenly seeing that car on the road seemingly everywhere you go. They were probably always there, but because your experiences have changed, you now notice them whereas you may not have before.

The "assisted" protocols (Clomid/Menopur/IUI/IVF) are complex in that they give couples deep insights into what it takes to influence a positive pregnancy outcome. I stop at influence and do not use the guarantee because these measures essentially amount to putting the boat in the water. It doesn't mean that the boat (the pregnancy) is without holes (some flaw or flaws) that will cause it to sink (the pregnancy failing). Let's take the Clomid protocol, for example. With Clomid, the doctor gives the woman medication in pill form that's designed to cause the pituitary gland to secrete more Follicle Stimulating Hormone (FSH), which causes one or more ovarian follicles containing eggs to grow fast. If a Clomid cycle is successful, eggs are released from the ovary (with or without a trigger shot) and ovulation occurs.

There's all sorts of routine monitoring that comes with this option. The couples get to see the follicles on the ultrasound screen and watch the doctor log their measurements. These are insights you don't get when "doing it the old-fashioned way." Eventually the doctor makes a determination that one or more of the follicles are mature enough and usually makes a recommendation to trigger ovulation with a trigger shot, which is an HCG hormone surge that helps the egg(s) release from the follicle. Usually couples are given instructions to go home and "do the baby dance" and hope for the best in a few weeks when they do a pregnancy test.

With the Menopur/Follistim protocol, it's usually accompanied by a round of Clomid. The Menopur further stimulates the ovaries to grow quickly. The main thing I remember my wife saying about the Menopur injection was that it burned going in. Menopur tends to be used with Intrauterine Insemination (IUI) cycles and egg retrievals for IVF. In an egg retrieval scenario, you want to stimulate as many follicles as possible to maximize how many eggs are retrieved for fertilization. This option is pretty grueling, as the home stretch of a stimulation cycle is uncomfortable for the woman because her ovaries are full of many stimulated eggs. It is, I would imagine, very similar to the home stretch of a pregnancy where the woman is ready to be relieved of the "occupant(s)" that has been growing in her uterus.

On top of this, in the IUI and IVF scenarios, the woman (or her surrogate) must take additional medications to prepare her uterus to be in the best position to receive an embryo or embryos. This also involves injections, a progesterone regimen (either vaginal suppositories or progesterone in oil given via intramuscular injection), ultrasound monitoring and bloodwork to ensure that hormone levels are exactly where they should be or at least in expected ranges. In my opinion, this stage can sometimes be compromised by a difficult egg retrieval recovery. Sometimes the trigger shot causes the ovaries to be overstimulated, which causes discomfort and bloating. To me, it seems that this puts additional strain on the woman's body, which is expected to turn around and recover in time to "host" an embryo and ultimately a viable pregnancy. Angelique did not recover sufficiently from her egg retrieval procedures, and usually was still experiencing discomfort from the procedure after undergoing the embryo transfer.

The Social Aspect of a Pregnancy Journey

There is a tremendous social aspect associated with any given pregnancy journey, specifically when it comes to a couple struggling with infertility. Infertility challenges are nothing new, as they have been going on for centuries; however, with the advent of the Internet, information can be dispersed in record time. Revolutionary social media platforms such as Facebook and YouTube are like kerosene to a flame, adding fuel to the fire, and it generally stinks. They allow people, whether it be family, friends or complete strangers, to meddle in someone's business if couples struggling with infertility don't take the proper precautions. The social aspect of a pregnancy journey is usually when couples or individuals first encounter triggers, and the triggers tend to get worse as the prospects of success diminish. Below are some areas that this chapter will focus on from both the male and female perspective.

Sharing the News

What exactly is "the news"? It really depends on where you are in your journey. The first place to start is informing others that you are trying to conceive or officially "trying". Usually couples keep it close to the vest (usually close friends or family) before opening up to others about their efforts to conceive. It's a very personal matter, and it's embarrassing because it seems like something that should be very easy to accomplish.

The other form of "the news" is learning that someone else is pregnant. Sharing this particular news is always more fun than hearing it when you're struggling to conceive a baby, and even more so for the woman in the equation. On the flip side, couples struggling to conceive that finally do get pregnant tend to make "rookie mistakes" and share the news far too early (in the first trimester, when the chances of miscarriage are relatively high for many). If a miscarriage occurs, an unshakable embarrassment takes over and the couple now finds itself having to explain what happened and why (tough to say why), and if they didn't tell anyone about it, they must process the loss and try and pretend like nothing happened to avoid questions. As the journey drags on, you tend to wear your pain and sorrow, and people tend to notice you're not quite yourself.

Sharing the news is unfortunately a common time for folks who mean well and are only trying to help to "step in it" and say something either inappropriate or insensitive. This causes couples or the "sharer" of the news to withdraw and essentially try and go at it alone, which only makes matters worse because a feeling of isolation takes over and the person feels they are the only one in the world experiencing this.

Fortunately, the Internet community of couples trying to conceive is a good source of reference for many. The caveat is that couples can drive themselves crazy researching an issue they may be experiencing in their own journey in an attempt to learn what the outcome might be. This is especially true when couples "graduate" to IVF—trust me, no IVF cycle is the same. Each has its twists and turns. The most important thing for couples to figure out is what to share and not share. It's not a good idea sharing any information you're not comfortable with. The couple owns the feelings associated with their own journey. These feelings cannot be ignored, either. Moving forward, wounded, is hard enough. Emotional strength must be reserved for the real fight. Talking too much about your struggles is unhealthy. It's best to vent and get back to being positive. Infertility struggles tend to make couples feel somewhat inadequate, and who really wants to advertise this? It's an embarrassing reality that a lot of people are ashamed of. Social media can do more harm than good as a result.

Managing Opinions and Expectations

Outsiders looking in on a couple's infertility journey often have opinions about what's going on or what should be done, and it's important for couples to recognize this. This is typically where opinions about how to "make it happen", with the "it" being the child, surface. Depending on how couples share the information, they usually end up being told that they should go on vacation, relax or simply adopt (as if it's that simple). This book was written the way it was because—wait for it—IT'S NOT THAT EASY! There are many different opinions that come into play: the opinions of friends can either be the most relevant or the most hurtful.

People you thought were your friends usually brag about how easy it was for them. People who are truly your friends do what good friends should when they learn of a couple's struggles—LISTEN. An infertility struggle is hard enough to divulge. Opinions can still be put out there, but there's a constructive way of presenting them without hurting feelings. This is extremely tough, as a majority of folks speak before they think. There's that saying about walking a mile in someone else's shoes…

Family opinions are also very hard to cope with. From the husband/male perspective, there's a pride factor. The opinion from family members may surface as a question, such as, "Why can't you get this done?" or "What's wrong with your wife?"

The woman in the equation doesn't have it any easier. The ability to bear children is a hidden expectation in many families. This is where you hear the question, "When are you going to give me grandchildren?" Once the family members have learned the news that a couple is actively trying to have a baby, a question from parents (hopefully they only have thought it and not asked directly) is likely, "Why can't you give me grandchildren?" Now that's pressure!

Expectations tend to be an issue when family are aware of infertility struggles and a sense of urgency is created that shouldn't be there. Somebody's old and might not be around much longer, or someone else's kids are nearly grown now (congratulations!). Or a woman is told by her sister that all her husband has to do is look at her and she's pregnant. Pregnancy becomes a race of sorts. A woman's biological clock may start to tick for a variety of reasons—advanced maternal age is not always the primary driver.

The Word "Journey", and Why Some Hate It

A journey has a both a beginning and an end. An infertility journey is meant to symbolize the process associated with having a baby, and unfortunately it's far from straightforward. All couples, once they realize that something is not right along the way of their quest to have a family, hope that it won't take them very long to have a baby. The general rule of thumb is that it should happen within six months or so of officially "trying". I watched a vlog (video blog) on YouTube where someone openly expressed their outright disgust with the word "journey" with respect to infertility struggles. The simple fact is that it's a journey, whether one wants to admit it or not. From this person's perspective, they probably felt like something was wrong with them for having to be on this particular path at all. They were just starting out, having one unsuccessful IVF cycle under their belts, and pretty much wanted to steer clear of any words like journey that would imply a long struggle.

Every couple's infertility struggle is very personal. With each failure or unsuccessful attempt, the idea of hopping back on that path becomes that much more difficult, especially for a woman and specifically with IVF. An IVF cycle, specifically a cycle that also includes an egg retrieval, is very hard on a woman's body. The amount of preparation, sacrifice (if one enjoys consuming alcohol), pain, hormonal changes and anxiety quickly become a point of intimidation when talk starts of trying again (continuing on the journey). Some couples, in their quest to have a baby, choose to repeatedly go through this. My question is, if and when you find success (especially with that path), how can you not use the word journey? Depending on the reason for the infertility, it often can take folks years to find success.

Maybe the reluctance to associate the word "journey" with infertility comes from a deep-rooted fear that there may not be an end. That's actually a flawed assumption, unless options are extremely limited out the gate. An example of this would be insisting that the baby has to be biologically related to BOTH parents. Another extreme would be giving up completely and choosing to go childless.

Journeys happen along paths. I remember very clearly during an IVF consultation with a doctor we'd worked with a few times previously, the doctor said something at the end of the consultation that stuck with my wife Angelique and me. We had taken a one-year break between our previous cycle and the one we were about to do in the summer of 2013, and the doctor said, "Pick a path, and stay on it." When we had hopped off the path during this break, we tried natural homeopathic therapies like hormone balancing, juicing and vegetarian diets. The other part of this message was that we were running out of time. Angelique was thirty-eight years old at the time, and the doctor made that statement in response to the known fact that egg quality declines after age thirty-five and it's that much more difficult to get pregnant because there are significantly more abnormal embryos.

After that consultation, we wondered how long our journey would actually be. It ended up going on for another one and a half years or so before it reached a successful conclusion.

When you find yourself struggling with infertility, you become very acquainted with the stages of grief, and it's very difficult to reach **acceptance**. It's hard to accept that this struggle you find yourself in is the hand of cards you were dealt to play with. It really isn't fair that so many couples have to struggle with this, but couples that do have many decisions to make. For example:

- Do we keep trying the old-fashioned way? And for how long before we pursue other options?
- How many Clomid cycles should we do before we move to IUI?
- How many IUI cycles should we do?
- We are frustrated that we haven't gotten pregnant, should we just do IVF?
- There's something wrong with my eggs. Should we use donor eggs and try to find success that way?
- We have been diagnosed with male factor infertility. Should we use donor sperm and is my husband willing to do that?
- It's been determined that I can't carry a pregnancy. Should we pursue a gestational surrogate, and can we afford it?

- None of our IVF cycles have worked, yet we still have frozen embryos. Should we continue to try and use them or do another fresh IVF cycle?
- Should we just adopt?

As you can see, there are many decisions that couples often find themselves faced with—these are all potential paths couples choose from during their infertility journey.

Maybe using the word "journey" hurts some because it implies that it will be a long process—too long, actually. Each path takes time and, unfortunately, none of them guarantee success. Choosing to continue and keep fighting implies acknowledging that there may be additional disappointments, frustrations, unknowns, twists and turns. "Regular" folks without fertility issues will continue to get pregnant all around you, and babies will continue to be born—that's just the cycle of life at work. When you're struggling with infertility, you become hypersensitive to things like that, so it's quite possible that using a word like "journey" doesn't feel appropriate when you don't even want to be on that path.

From my perspective, the journey is what you make it. It's not meant to be pleasant, easy, cheap, fun, exciting or without bumps. There's also no magic formula for success. There are paths, but they offer a chance at your dream—nothing more, nothing less.

I personally think that the word journey is a positive word and should not be substituted. After all, nothing worth having comes easy. Rich (I'm talking about the really rich—the billionaires) people usually acquire their wealth by way of hard work and determination over a period of time, and accumulate a series of failures before finding success.

On the path to a baby, there is usually adversity that must be overcome. There's personal sacrifice, but the greatest challenge is the emotional beating you take with each failure. While I feel strongly that journey is the right word, I can't say there is any magic formula as far as quantifying it or measuring it. What's the right answer here? Is it in terms of total years, or is it in how many things a couple has tried along the way?

For example, is a couple's journey to a baby that was one and a half years any less meaningful than someone whose journey was eight years? Is graduating to IVF the benchmark? I don't think any two journeys are the same, so they really shouldn't be compared. The same is true of how the journey comes to an end. A baby that's biologically related to both parents is not more significant than one where an egg donor was used or where the couple elected to adopt. At the end of the day, one would hope that the true significance is found in how much the child is loved by both parents.

I do think it's important for couples that find success to spend some time reflecting about what they accomplished. Social media gives many families opportunities to do that, because there's always someone struggling with infertility. A family might stumble upon a picture of a baby in the Neonatal Intensive Care Unit (NICU) and be reminded of their own NICU stay, causing them to relive that time, find their own pictures and share them. The biggest benefit of reflecting is that it reminds you to be sensitive to what someone might be going through.

Of all of the things Angelique and I ended up trying on our own path to having a family of our own, I'm astounded by how common a problem infertility is. Just look at the various online forums—the struggle is very real. I once stumbled upon a thread where a woman was on her tenth IVF cycle (all fresh), had been trying ten years and still didn't have a baby. I can imagine that must have been brutal. It gets so hard to stay strong as time goes on, and I wonder, emotionally, what the true impact is on both the man and the woman in the equation. Perhaps there's some healing that takes place if you're lucky to have a baby as a result of your collective efforts, but it's still worth pondering. An infertility journey isn't easy to survive, either—I can see why it's easier to give up, as the disappointment intensifies with each failure (and who likes to fail repeatedly?). Some couples end up divorced—I don't pretend to know all of the reasons, but I do know that it happens often.

Interestingly enough, writing this chapter made that song *Don't Stop Believin'* by—guess who?—Journey pop into my head. Maybe that's what the hidden message is—no matter what the outcome, don't stop believing. The lyrics aren't completely applicable, but it's the thought that counts, right?

Angelique's Pregnancy

Angelique's triplet pregnancy started out with a **BANG**. As the blood test results came in, we noticed that the HGC (pregnancy hormone) numbers were very high—in fact, they were higher than we'd ever seen before, so we knew we likely had more than one baby in the mix. It was still not cause for celebration for us, however. After all, we'd been through this before—five previous IVF cycles—and had learned to brace ourselves for disappointment.

We had transferred four embryos, so it's very likely all four took initially. Somehow, Angelique battled nausea, but never heaved the entire pregnancy—lucky her.

When it was time to learn whether or not Angelique was pregnant, I remember we were both at work (we worked for the same department at the time) and I got the call from the IVF clinic. The nurse who called was really excited, so I knew it was good. I told the nurse I needed to place her on hold while I went to go get my wife and put my phone on mute, and since Angelique was just a stone's throw away from my office, I went and grabbed her and asked her to close the office door behind her. Then I took the phone off mute and asked the nurse to deliver the news to us both.

Angelique instantly burst into tears when she heard "congratulations" and I gave her a big hug. When she heard the initial beta number of 1,563, I think she responded, "Holy Shit!"

I could see the look of relief on her face after she got the news. This IVF cycle was different for a few reasons. Over the course of the previous five IVF cycles, she had learned to put her mind and body on autopilot just to get through the whole ordeal. For this sixth cycle, she not only had to do that, but she had to put her faith and trust in the hands of a generous egg donor, yet take back control of her body and prepare it to receive these four embryos. This was out of her hands, but then again, it wasn't.

After the call, Angelique sat in my office seated at the round table with her eyes closed, and she rocked back and forth with tears running down her face and a slight smile. I knew what she was reflecting on. After the embryos were transferred, it was a waiting game like no other. She was afraid to move. She camped out in the bed in the hotel room, and, over the next few days, only got up when absolutely necessary. She really wanted the transferred embryos to stick this time. It had been suggested that she eat lots of pineapple, so we got some from Whole Foods after the embryo transfer. Was that the X-factor? Who knows? Once the next few blood test results came back over the subsequent few days, we had a feeling this was going to be our cycle and that it would finally work.

We had both learned to not read too much into the numbers by this time. For example, it's easy to obsess about how high (or low) the number might be and take to Google to see what others have experienced on discussion threads. It becomes almost second nature to over-analyze the results. I remember in our earlier IVF cycles obsessing about "doubling times" where the HCG level was, in theory, supposed to double every forty-eight hours, as this was one possible sign that the pregnancy was progressing normally and might be viable.

With this final cycle, something told me not to dwell on doubling times. Given that it was likely multiples, it made sense for us to not put much stock in that because we transferred four embryos and all four embryos may have initially implanted (wow—what a thought).

I wanted to mention this because of the information found on the chart below. Note the doubling times—not quite forty-eight hours.

Here is the table and chart depicting the HCG rise for Angelique's successful IVF cycle:

DATE	BETA LEVEL	INCREASE	48-HOUR LEVEL	96-HOUR LEVEL	DOUBLING TIME (HOURS)
5/1/2014	1,563	1,563	3,126	6,252	--
5/3/2014	3,075	1,512	6,150	12,300	49.2
5/10/2014	32,973	29,898	65,946	131,892	49.1

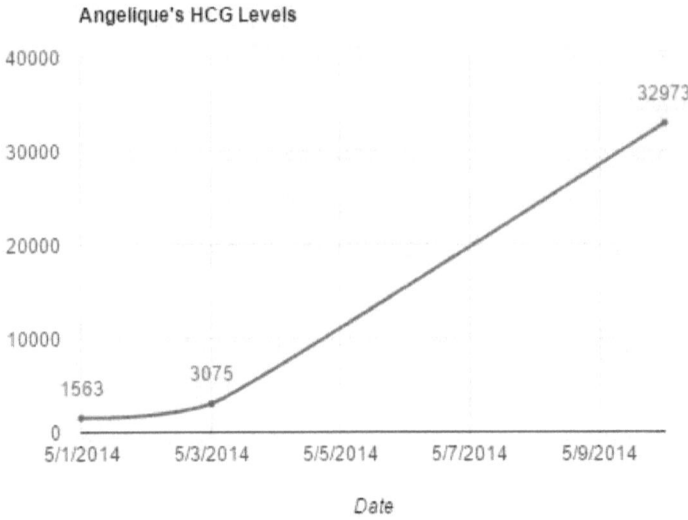

The six-week ultrasound confirmed what we had suspected—not only was it definitely multiples, but it was triplets. The doctor's response was, "When it rains, it pours."

We were beyond thrilled—we finally had some better odds to work with and weren't regretting our decision to put in all four embryos. We'd gone through this too many times to risk transferring only one, so we upped the stakes and accepted the risks.

I'd like to provide some additional context regarding our decision to transfer all four embryos. On the actual day of the April 2014 embryo transfer, our IVF doctor had joined us in the embryo transfer room and gave us the results of our remaining embryos. He mentioned that we had four to work with—two were outstanding quality, and the other two could go either way. He also gave us recommendations on how many to transfer, although the final choice was ours to make. We had always transferred two embryos before, but that wasn't working for us. He had mentioned that, given the 50/50 status of the other two embryos, we could transfer them or freeze them, but explained that there was no guarantee that either embryo would survive the freezing process.

So, there Angelique and I sat after Dr. Kolb left the room to give us time to discuss our options. We talked about the risks of transferring all four and all of them taking, but Angelique looked me in the eyes and said, "I can do this. I want to do at least three. You know what, let's put them all in and see what happens."

My only question to her was, "Are you sure?" to which she replied, "Honey, how many more times do you want to keep going through this?"

The answer to that question was zero, and that made it an easier decision, as far as how to proceed was concerned.

Once she saw how high her initial HCG numbers were and how they continued their meteoric rise, Angelique's confidence was starting to skyrocket—she was beginning to believe in her ability to do this and have a hopeful outlook. She started showing about week seven. Her appetite increased, too. She had a craving for Taco Bell pretty much every day, and it was clear her body was requiring more and more fuel and was gearing up for something big. By week nine, she was sporting a beautiful bump.

This is when the "complaining" really took off. I would hear every day, a couple of times a day, how tired she was. She could barely keep her eyes open. It was triplets, so one could safely assume that they were sucking the life force out of her in order to grow big and strong. It would seem that every evening, around five or six o'clock, the babies would start their growing, as she'd have cramping and could feel things stretching out. But it was most noticeable on Sunday evenings, and Monday morning she'd wake up and look noticeably, well...bigger.

We elected to keep flying her down to Pasadena for the remaining ultrasounds until the doctor was ready to release her. We could have paid extra money and stayed local and done the remote monitoring, but we loved Dr. Kolb's bedside manner, and it was important for me to keep Angelique's spirits up in the early stages of the pregnancy. Being around Dr. Kolb and his team did just that. She'd fly in to Burbank, hail an Uber car to the IVF clinic, have her ultrasound and bloodwork, stop at Whole Foods, hail an Uber car back to the airport, and fly back to Sacramento.

As we neared being released from Dr. Kolb's care, we faced a decision: stopping progesterone and estrogen supplements. Angelique had been on these since the embryo transfer and, given that the previous cycle revealed lower-than-normal levels of progesterone, she felt very dependent on the two supplements and wondered if the placenta(s) would take over or if the pregnancy would fail without them. She was very reluctant to stop taking the supplements, as she was worried that the placentas would not take over and that she would lose the pregnancies. A conversation with Dr. Kolb put her concerns at ease. She ended up stopping the supplements at about ten weeks and trusting that everything would be fine—and it was. It wouldn't have hurt her continuing on, but it was still a difficult decision that she wrestled with, and I really can't fault her for being conflicted about stopping the supplements, given the history that was in play. It had been a long journey and it was very difficult for her to believe that this would actually work this time.

I did everything I possibly could to support her throughout this pregnancy. My role shifted from co-managing the entire IVF cycle with our egg donor, including all of the medications she needed to take, to figuring out how to keep Angelique as comfortable as possible. I catered to her every need—she was carrying precious cargo! She would get hungry in an instant, so she had to have food handy. Early on in the pregnancy, though, the only thing that was sounding good was buttered and toasted sourdough bread. The thought of anything else made her queasy, so that's what she'd eat. She also kept a supply of candied ginger nearby to calm the nausea. You try cooking for someone that turns her nose up at everything you propose, even the things that used to sound good—it's an impossible task, that's for sure.

Once we hit ten weeks, things seemed to go on autopilot. Angelique's belly grew rapidly, and soon she was experiencing shortness of breath. We kept waiting for something major to happen, but it didn't, until week seventeen.

Leading up to week seventeen, I watched as she started to "own" the pregnancy and believe. We were very focused on the details of her care, being back under the services of Kaiser Permanente Hospital for her pregnancy care. It was a weird feeling being treated as an ordinary pregnancy when we still felt vulnerable. No more routine ultrasounds unless there were complications—it really was blind faith. This was standard protocol for IVF cycles. Dr. Kolb released Angelique from his care and she had to get an initial ultrasound from her OB/GYN (Obstetrics and Gynecology) before being referred to the high-risk pregnancy doctor.

I tried explaining Angelique's history to the new OB/GYN doctor, but this doctor didn't seem to grasp the magnitude of the details, let alone the concerns. In fact, it didn't make sense to explain it to this doctor because the ultimate goal was to hand Angelique off to the perinatologist, as they were the most experienced with managing high-risk pregnancies. Therefore, I really didn't read much into it. By the time we got to the high-risk pregnancy doctor, things got interesting. They were nice, but also had an easy-going approach to their job that didn't necessarily sit well with either of us.

Fortunately, there was another perinatologist, Dr. Edward Mentakis, that we saw when our primary wasn't available, and we both really liked him, especially the fact that he was overly concerned about the details of our pregnancy and we appreciated that "better safe than sorry" attitude. Differences in approaches to care aside, Angelique and I had both learned to lower our expectations and tune out what are really nice-to-haves in favor of delivering the results we were looking for (healthy babies).

The "fun" in Angelique's pregnancy began on August 8, 2014. We went in for a routine perinatologist check-up and we got Dr. Mentakis, the doctor who was filling in for our primary perinatologist. He performed the ultrasound, got really quiet as he measured the length of Angelique's cervix, pulled out the ultrasound wand and cleaned up.

Angelique and I had left our jobs for a few hours fully intending to go back after the appointment. The doctor casually asked Angelique, "Are you still working?" She was seventeen weeks pregnant at the time and responded, "Yep."

He quickly fired back, "Not anymore...here's why." He then printed out ultrasound pictures of her cervix and explained in great detail what the problem was. It was far too short to sustain the pregnancy over the long term, and there was also cervical funneling. Cervical funneling is a sign of cervical incompetence, meaning the cervix is compromised and capable of contributing to preterm delivery.

Before we freaked out, Dr. Mentakis explained that he was putting Angelique on strict bed rest for the remainder of the pregnancy, and that he was scheduling her for an emergency procedure later that evening called a cerclage. He explained that he was going to insert a stitch in the cervix to keep it closed, and that the hope was the stitch would hold and keep the water bag from breaking and causing pre-term labor as a result of the babies getting heavier over the remainder of the pregnancy.

We came back for the procedure later that evening after going home for a few hours. The procedure was a quick one—about fifteen minutes in total, and a few hours of recovery time. After the procedure was over, the doctor came out and explained that he actually put two stitches in to make sure things would hold, and then he gave us discharge instructions. Angelique was in considerable pain afterwards. Dr. Mentakis must have been tugging on those stitches pretty hard (to ensure that they were inserted properly) as that was the first thing Angelique asked me when she felt the pain. The nurses gave her Tylenol in an IV for the pain, but that didn't work.

Next the nurses tried morphine, but that didn't work for her either, so they finally gave her Delota, to which she gave the nurse that administered it a thumbs up, and she finally started to relax. Before they gave her the Delota, she was crying and pushing because it hurt so badly, though they told her not to push. I had horrible thoughts running through my head of the babies coming, and I knew that it was way too early for any of them to survive. You can imagine how relieved I was when the Delota worked and, as she neared discharge from the hospital in the middle of the night, she was back to her chipper self.

The follow-up appointment a few days later went well. The ultrasound revealed that the funneling had subsided and that the stitches were doing their job. However, at each subsequent ultrasound appointment, Angelique began to obsess about the cervical length measurement. There was nothing I could do to prevent her from doing that—she knew how much was riding on those stitches holding. The number would fluctuate—mostly decreasing—and she would get concerned. The doctor never seemed worried about it.

Seven more weeks went by with me managing her care, making sure she stayed off her feet as much as possible before our next scare. We had reached twenty-four weeks in the pregnancy, and went to the perinatologist for routine ultrasound. At the conclusion of the ultrasound, we were advised to head over to the hospital, as Angelique had a very sharp pain during the ultrasound.

When we got there, it turned out Angelique was experiencing preterm labor. Scary stuff, I tell you. The contractions got worse, and the labor and delivery doctor explained to us that they were going to try to get the contractions to stop by giving Angelique fluids, but that she would be getting a steroid shot to help the babies' lungs develop should they come early (like that day).

Neither of us were prepared for that potential reality, by the way. Yes, it's true that twenty-four weeks is generally considered viability for pregnancy and is a major milestone. Viability essentially means that a baby born that early could potentially survive with *significant* medical help, and the chances of complications and/or long-term disabilities are very high.

We ended up having to sign a bunch of paperwork in case the babies came. We met our potential C-section surgeon and some of the nurses and surgical team members just in case. There was talk of permanently admitting Angelique for the duration of the pregnancy (eight to ten more weeks). Believe it or not, we were both actually OK with this, as she would be in the ideal place should anything go wrong—and she could opt out of eating hospital food. Angelique's mom met us at the hospital. Angelique was hooked up to monitoring equipment to keep an eye on the babies' vitals.

We got lucky that day, and Angelique was discharged the following day after getting a second steroid shot. From there, it was back home to be cooped up in a dark room for the remainder of the pregnancy. This period of the pregnancy was very challenging for her. She'd get very hungry quickly, yet run out of room in her stomach shortly after she started eating. She drank many protein shakes and ate a lot of eggs. She would sleep most of the day and watch Netflix, but her schedule was completely off. I had a miniature fridge outside of her room stocked with yogurts, soups, protein shakes and whatever else sounded good to her. Her walking range was limited—to the bathroom, miniature fridge and back to bed.

Two days a week her mom would come and change out the sheets, so she got to sit in the living room for a while until her sheets were changed. That was pretty much the highlight of her weeks. Loneliness ensued (and how could it not?). She had a friend Diane who would come by and spend a few hours with her several days a week, and this companionship was a life saver. It was refreshing for Angelique to not be alone with her thoughts and saddled with this monumental task of carrying triplets as long as she possibly could.

We had an opportunity during the pregnancy to enjoy the experience, believe it or not. I started a list of potential baby names before we knew what the genders would be. We had a good list of names, and eventually settled on Michaela Brielle and Emma Grace if we had more than one girl, and Christopher William and Owen Matthew if we ended up with more than one boy.

While she could still move around, we took her in for a 3-D ultrasound in order to learn the genders of our three babies. The gender determination ultrasound revealed that we were having two girls and one boy. We decided to name the first girl Michaela Brielle, the second girl Emma Grace, and the boy Christopher William. There is a great deal of symbolism built into each name.

Michaela is a hybrid name that contains the letters "M" (Michael) and "A" (Angelique). The middle name, Brielle, is a tribute to my love of French names, but also gives the initial combination of "M-B-C". My mother and my sister and I all share the common initials of "M-B-C".

Emma was a name that Angelique and I both liked, and Grace seemed to pair nicely with it as a middle name. Emma also contains the symbolic letters "M" and "A". Christopher's name is a combination of the middle name of my older brother (Clinton Christopher Gaston), and the first name of my father (William Bernard Cave). These are two of the finest men I've known in my life.

As the weeks passed, Angelique got more and more physically uncomfortable, and let anyone who would listen know about it. Her hips hurt badly from having to lay on her side, and there really was no such thing as a comfortable position, as all three babies had issues with whatever position she found that was comfortable for her. Pair that with all of the constant movement in her belly and I'm surprised she didn't go insane.

Towards the end of the pregnancy, she got concerned because she could no longer feel Michaela move. By this time, Michaela, who was on the very bottom, had descended deep into Angelique's pelvic area and was running out of real estate.

We went in to the hospital's labor and delivery ward to get things checked out. What was interesting about this visit was that, as big as Angelique was, she didn't look like she was carrying triplets, so the nurses essentially told her to have a seat. She refused and attempted to find a bathroom because she had to go frequently with the weight of the babies pushing on her bladder. She tried to use the one that was steps away from the check-in area, and one of the nurses told her that it was for triage patients only. She explained that she was carrying triplets and couldn't wait any longer to find another restroom, and immediately, she had three nurses waiting on her hand and foot, finding her a transport cart and suddenly very concerned. It was hilarious.

They hooked Angelique up to all of the baby monitors again, and the babies kept kicking each other's monitors offline, so we were there for hours. Eventually a doctor came in and felt it was best to do an ultrasound to see for sure what was going on. There were three heartbeats, and this is when we saw that Michaela's placenta was blocking all of her kicks. She was kicking like crazy, but the placenta was absorbing the kicks and preventing Angelique from feeling her moving around. Once Angelique saw that, she was relieved and so was I. We went home and didn't come back to the hospital until three or so more weeks for another routine checkup. Things got real then.

Before each appointment, Angelique had to provide a urine sample. This was to test for protein in the urine, which is a sign of preeclampsia. Angelique passed both of the glucose tests she did, so she avoided gestational diabetes, but her results came back with elevated protein levels. The doctor told us that she wanted to monitor the levels more closely and told Angelique to come back the following day (October 23, 2014) to give another urine sample and have the babies hooked up to the monitors again. If everything checked out, we had a growth ultrasound scheduled for later that afternoon. The results came back with the levels being even higher, so there was concern that Angelique had developed preeclampsia.

The labor and delivery doctor informed us that we could be delivering babies that day. Upon hearing those words, things became very real for us. Angelique had to sit up to have the monitoring done and was getting increasingly uncomfortable and complaining of back pain. Contractions started. They checked her cervix and she was one centimeter dilated. The labor and delivery nurses determined that they weren't going to be able to stop the contractions and the labor and delivery doctor made arrangements with the surgical team for a C-section.

This was one of the most beautifully coordinated efforts I had ever seen. Angelique was taken upstairs from the triage area, and into a room similar to the one we were in during the twenty-four week pre-term labor scare. We met the NICU nurse team and the surgery doctor, and signed paperwork again. This was really happening. I texted Angelique's parents, notified my employer that our babies were coming, texted my mom, and then essentially went dark for a while until the babies were born.

I was there in the operating room for their birth. There was a huge team of nurses—at least six—at three stations. Angelique was given a spinal tap, and she threw up for the first time throughout her entire pregnancy. It all happened so fast. The next thing I knew, they pulled our daughter Michaela out of Angelique's womb at 12:27 p.m. I didn't hear any crying, but saw them cart her off to a table and hover over her. Next up was our daughter Emma at 12:28 p.m. She squealed and Angelique started crying. I saw Emma and that head full of hair, and then the nurses hovered over her at her station. At 12:30 p.m., they pulled out our son Christopher. Apparently, he was hanging on to Angelique's rib, probably negotiating with the surgeons to close her back up and leave him in to bake a little longer. He had been at the very top of her uterus, in the "penthouse", and had the freedom to move about the cabin. His squeal when they suctioned out his mouth and nose was legendary.

They picked up each baby and gave me the opportunity to see them. I tried to take pictures to show Angelique. Five or so minutes went by and she wondered what was wrong, as they were still trying to put her organs back inside her. They were having difficulty controlling the blood loss. The next thing I knew, I was kicked out of the operating room while they tended to her. Apparently, she had lost a lot of blood, but, she pulled through and I rejoined her in the recovery room about twenty minutes later. *That* was scary – we could have lost her.

Angelique did it, though. She not only had a child, but she carried triplets and they were all born a good size: 2 lbs. 8.9 oz., 2 lbs. 10 oz., and 2 lbs. 8.6 oz., respectively. When the nurses learned she was a vegetarian, they wondered how the babies were such a good size for twenty-nine weeks and three days without eating any meat. She informed them that there are many other sources of protein.

    After seven and a half years of frustration and sacrifice, Angelique finally had her reward—a family. Choosing a new path with IVF using donor eggs resulted in new beginnings for us. She really enjoyed being pregnant and was sad to see it come to an end. I'm glad the doctor put her on bed rest when he did. It was a reminder that there was something bigger in store for us both, and that we needed to do whatever it took to keep that as our focus. Growing three babies at once isn't easy, and neither is remaining calm when you have had the roller coaster ride we've had.

Triggers

In this context, triggers are events that cause unexplained emotions and reactions. You might think that, when it comes to couples struggling with infertility, only a woman can have triggers. Actually, men have triggers too, and they are just as painful. In this chapter, I will share a few of the triggers my wife Angelique and I both experienced over the course of our years trying to conceive. Many readers will be able to relate to this chapter because triggers are usually a product of frustrations boiling over, and everyone's triggers produce unique reactions. Even though we have three babies now, I've learned that I actually still have a few triggers.

For example, in the previous house that we owned a few years ago, a few blocks away from us there was a house that had been vacant, when a young couple moved in and pretty much kept to themselves for the better part of a year. I could tell they were newlyweds each time I walked by their home and saw them out front.

One day I was out for a walk, and I stopped to introduce myself and they confirmed they were just starting out and were newlyweds. For months I'd see them outside fixing up the house, but no child was ever seen with them. I would tell myself that they were just enjoying being married, though from what I had seen, a baby arrives within six months to a year of being married.

Over the course of our own struggles, each time I walked by this young couple's house, I found myself specifically checking to see if the woman had a bump. I never did see a bump, but over the course of the next six months, saw a baby in a stroller, so clearly they had no problems getting pregnant.

Although Angelique and I had found our own brand of success, I found myself a tad jealous that it was so easy for them to get pregnant. Seeing that baby represented a trigger for me—a reminder of my own journey. Fortunately, I wasn't angry or anything. It was more a brief period of reflection, and I felt that I could look back at certain aspects of our struggle and it didn't quite hurt as bad to replay them. I do wish it had been easier for us, though. However, nothing worth having is ever easy.

It's natural to feel envious of couples who seem to automatically get pregnant. Early on in our journey, I noticed that seeing these couples instantly find success reminded my wife that there was something wrong preventing us from sharing that joyous feeling of being pregnant. I recall her learning of a couple's news and being somewhat happy for them, but that quickly faded when the excitement expressed by the couple took on a new life, thanks to social media, specifically Facebook. As a result, Facebook quickly turned into a trigger. It seemed like at least once a week someone was announcing pregnancy news. When you're struggling, this stings—bad. This is what led Angelique to deactivate her account—she left her Facebook account deactivated for several years, actually. She used to routinely hover over my shoulder and check out what was happening on my own Facebook feed, but even that stopped, as seeing the success of others through pregnancy announcements on Facebook represented a painful reminder and as a result represented a trigger. Triggers produce a natural tendency to avoid—unfortunately, you can run but you can't hide.

Social media soon became a trigger for me as well. I didn't go as far as to deactivate my account, but I started to hide the "Friends" on Facebook that were announcing pregnancy news, as the more time dragged on, the harder it got. Before I knew it, my Facebook News Feed was very quiet having hidden posts from specific friends, preventing me from seeing any news about their pregnancies that they may have posted. I started this practice of hiding posts from friends after seeing photos of a newborn, and then watching children grow up before my eyes, all while realizing we still didn't have children of our own. It was what I needed to do in order to cope. I don't expect anyone to understand, but it was necessary to protect myself in order to carry on and keep from getting completely discouraged with how long it was taking. Over the years, I had hidden so many people from my Facebook feed that I thought people were done growing their families. Facebook was a way to stay connected and allows one to follow others without necessarily commenting. Reality is, it was a high-level trigger: I saw a pattern of people in their thirties all starting families around the same time, and parenthood was completely transforming them.

I even witnessed a few cruel April Fools' Day jokes along the way. At first, I didn't get it, probably because I was so focused on my own journey. The posts read "I'm 6 weeks and craving <something>!". There were so many responses to those posts where others initially were thinking that the poster was pregnant. The fact is that it wasn't funny and was generally insensitive. Nowadays, you see those that are familiar with the infertility struggle posting content in advance of April Fools' Day to remind folks that infertility is no laughing matter and to be mindful of others' misfortunes.

At least with social media, you had a choice and could take measures to avoid this particular trigger. The worst for us both, particularly after a miscarriage in an IVF cycle, was having to go out on the town and see pregnant women everywhere. For whatever reason they are more visible when you're in the midst of an infertility struggle, and I imagine it's because you want it so badly for yourself.

Angelique wanted no part of going to any baby stores when she was struggling with infertility. In those stores, you are surrounded by pregnant women with beautiful baby bumps, or you see "new families" with a newborn in a stroller. I must admit that it gave me great pleasure to see my wife walk into a baby store, pregnant and showing and actually confident that she belonged there as a legitimate member of the mothers-to-be club. The baby bump was the badge of honor.

The only positive trigger for me came after our first pregnancy loss. It was the smell of the IVF clinic room once we returned for our second IVF attempt, which was our first frozen embryo transfer. We had taken a short break before trying again, and the smell of the examination room was strangely comforting after the brief hiatus. We had spent so much time in the examination room with all of the examinations, monitoring ultrasounds, procedures and other hallmarks of an IVF cycle. The smell was sweet with a hint of medical equipment. When I first smelled it, I felt excited and motivated. With each whiff, I felt more confident that this would be the IVF cycle where we would find success. It felt good to be back on the path.

As the IVF failures mounted, though, I grew to detest the smell. I was tired of failing, embarrassed that we had to keep returning, and soon it became the signature smell of the unknown. It's amazing how a smell can trigger memories. Go figure, the same is true of our NICU experience after our babies arrived. The NICU has a distinct smell too, and we spent even more time there. But for the NICU it's the sounds that are another trigger.

A few years after we brought our children home from the NICU, I dropped off some photos I had printed of the kids for the NICU staff so that they could see how healthy they were and how much they had grown. I was given a temporary badge and allowed to go downstairs to the NICU ward where the babies are cared for. By the time I got downstairs, it was like I had never left and was still making daily trips to visit my own kids. As I made my way to the nurses' station to drop off the photos, I walked by the various rooms where the babies are kept (called "pods"), and saw all of the isolettes and cribs. I also heard the familiar sounds of the various machines going off. Specifically, I heard the Bolus feed (used to provide nutrition to babies via a nasal feeding tube), and the heart monitor machines. Part of it was comforting to hear at first, but that soon was replaced with all of the scary moments when those alarms were going off because a baby had stopped breathing and needed stimulation. It was a reminder (thanks to that trigger) of how precious each life is in those early NICU days and what an emotional roller coaster it is for new parents.

We consider ourselves one of the lucky families—we survived our NICU experience and got to go home with all of our children. I remember one family that wasn't so lucky. The NICU chews folks up and spits them out, and it's not always pretty. One morning, I went to the NICU before work to drop off breast milk for the babies and say hello to them, and all hell broke out on the other row with one of the babies that had been born at twenty-five weeks. The baby had stopped breathing and the stimulation wasn't working. The next thing I knew, there were at least eight different doctors surrounding the baby attempting to save it. The baby was very tiny so great care was being taken while life-saving measures were underway. I was actually washing my hands and stopped dead in my tracks and just watched. They were successful in their efforts to revive the baby but watching all of that really shook me up. After seeing that, I hated hearing that heart monitor alarm start dinging. I put myself in the parents' shoes. They weren't there, as it was early in the morning. It was a bad enough episode to where I'm sure they were called, but I'm glad I never got one of those calls for any of our children. In the coming years I would visit the hospital for various reasons (vitamins for the kids, their prescription medications, etc.), and would walk around the campus by where the NICU is located. There is a window very close to the path I routinely took to the pharmacy, and any time I would walk past that window I would get goosebumps because that NICU pod was the room my children called home for the first six to seven weeks of their lives. I'm always nostalgic when I walk past the NICU, as I remember what a grind it is. Sometimes I see a family loading their newborn into a car and I know that is a NICU graduate because the baby is usually too small for their outfit. The graduation cap the baby gets to wear after leaving is also a giveaway.

"Just Adopt."

Adoption is a proven path that helps couples realize their dreams of becoming parents. I'm going to share with you my thoughts on this topic. This chapter is called "Just Adopt" because this proved to be one of the most annoying things I heard from people who learned of our struggles in the trying-to-conceive department and it's essentially a heartless thing to say to a couple that usually isn't well thought out. For me, it was also a trigger. When I heard this, I would usually check out of the conversation.

You see, it's not that simple. Every time I heard this from folks, they could barely elaborate when I asked them to. It was stated as the final solution and often sold as stress-free. Anyone who has adopted knows that isn't the case. When you commit to adoption, you go all in emotionally, and sometimes curveballs are thrown. For example, sometimes one of the parents contests the adoption, and a messy legal battle ensues. Worth pointing out is the fact that most people who mentioned these words usually meant well. But when the scars associated with multiple unsuccessful pregnancy attempts are in the mix, the words end up being perceived as condescending, insensitive and cruel. When you haven't had to struggle with infertility, you don't know what you don't know. You don't know how much weight those words carry when said to someone who is struggling. They are a dagger right to the heart.

I recall a conversation with my wife over dinner one night in 2007. She had asked me to give some thought to adopting a child, as she felt that we had a lot to offer a child. I don't think, back then, she knew something that I didn't or anything like that, but I promised her that I would take the time to think about it, which I did. I took a few years to think about it, actually, and I believe my official answer was that I was open to it but wanted us to have one of our own first. This was a year into our marriage—things were different back then. We would have never imagined the emotional roller coaster we'd soon find ourselves on.

Back then, we had this notion that we would be one of the 'normal' couples that got pregnant within six months of trying. We were certain that if we stayed the course, it would all work out. Grappling with infertility is like being stuck in a terrible maze—a maze that has twists, turns, dead ends and false hopes. When you're stuck in the maze, it's hard to see what's beyond it (the big picture). Perhaps some people assume that it's as easy as stating that a woman shouldn't put her body through all of the injections, procedures, etc. when there are so many children that are already born and in need of good homes and loving parents. Again, a person's right to choose notwithstanding, one cannot discredit the importance of a quality match between child and parent. Adoption is a long process, and when you're struggling with infertility, you

"JUST ADOPT."

naturally lack patience.

I'm not against adoption at all—after considerable deliberation, though, I personally came to the conclusion that it wasn't, for me, the primary option. Not everyone is cut out for a long, drawn-out struggle to conceive, and that's OK—we can only take so much heartbreak in our lives before we do whatever is necessary to protect ourselves from further suffering. I believe that two things are in play: pride *(I need to do this, whether I really can or not)* and primal instincts (the natural urge to want to procreate).

Most times, the third-party suggestion offered up to just adopt is thrown out there without any consideration for the individuals that actually have to make the decision—the parents-to-be. Their feelings, wishes and expectations.

Every situation is different. It seemed that anytime I told people that I didn't want to adopt, I became the bad guy, and I didn't think that this was fair at all. Last time I checked, it was a personal choice, and in my opinion one you don't make lightly. I even had people insist that I change my position, yet none of these people really knew me at all. (Side note: None of those people wrote me a check for $40,000 for adopting a child—nobody's that nice.)

I know several wonderful people who have adopted children, and it worked out for them; I've also seen situations where it didn't work out. For me, it boiled down to what would make me happy. Why would I do something that didn't make me happy? That wouldn't have been fair to the child at all and certainly not to Angelique. Children can sense things.

For me, it was extremely important that there be a biological connection. I'm sure this happens with couples that are faced with this decision, but I didn't think that my wife Angelique would dictate that we had to adopt because her eggs were preventing her from having a biological connection with the child(ren). Essentially, that would have translated into, "If I can't have a biological connection with the child(ren), neither can you."

By this time, we knew that egg quality was likely an issue. There wasn't an issue with my sperm. If there were, that would have been a different discussion.

Thanks to egg donation, at least a partial biological connection became a legitimate option for us. It was the ultimate compromise—it provided her with the opportunity to carry a pregnancy herself (which she did successfully), and I ended up with the biological connection that I wanted. I also wanted to know the donor and be comfortable with her, which I do and I am. It was a compromise because egg donation is essentially an egg adoption—ideally it would have been nice for Angelique to also have a biological connection, but it wasn't worth her risking maintaining that position and ending up with no children at all. She is their mother—period. She's the only mother whom they know, and she is the one who grew them in her body and made their lives possible. She is the one they go to when they are scared, and she's the one they call "Mommy".

The eggs that were donated put her on the path that worked, and she carried three babies herself, which proved that donor egg was the best path for her. The evidence surrounding an egg quality issue was clear in the form of five previous unsuccessful IVF fresh and frozen cycles. We never analyzed any of the embryos to determine if the root cause could be known through checking for chromosomal and genetic abnormalities, and we'll likely never know.

I'm certain there was a grieving process of sorts involved for Angelique as she was not able to attain success with her own eggs; however, we both remembered seeing the higher success statistics surrounding egg donation during a presentation at the IVF clinic we switched to—the success rates for egg donation made it clear that it was likely our best option moving forward, given everything we had tried. I wanted to see her find success with this process—she deserved to be rewarded for her efforts over the years. I saw the egg donation approach give her a renewed sense of hope, and she began to believe in herself again. It was a calculated risk, but one that paid off huge dividends, times three.

Angelique has a huge heart. She was always open to adoption. While we didn't see eye to eye on that topic, we respected each other's positions. She loves our triplets unconditionally and there is a very strong bond there. She wasn't forced by me to do something she was opposed to. She looked at the data, evaluated her options and, through the egg donation path, was able to see the big picture and a light at the end of the tunnel. The rest is history—it was absolutely the best decision for our situation.

You've probably heard many stories of couples that have decided to adopt and then BOOM!!! They get pregnant on their own naturally. Why is that? It's probably because if there is true acceptance with the decision, the woman finally relaxes (the pressure is off), or maybe it's truly random. In a way, some of the stresses associated with infertility are relieved; however, they can be replaced by potentially unpleasant aspects of the adoption process that could arise, such as delays, legal issues, etc.

I don't see adoption as an inferior option at all. Again, I have met some wonderful people who have adopted and are over the moon about the decision. It doesn't just change the child's life—it changes the parents' lives, too. A DNA connection isn't required to develop a loving bond, let alone to be considered a parent. Family, love and bonding take on all forms.

I would suggest that the recommendation to adopt not be made by friends and family—it's not helpful. It's an option capable of delivering benefits just like the others, and it has risks and costs as well. I know a few people who have adopted children and my observation is that they are equally as happy with their decision as they would be if the child were biologically theirs. I don't know all the factors that led to their decision, but I can see the love they provide and how happy they make their child, and that's what really matters.

Angelique and I chose *not* to donate our leftover frozen embryos. The rationale behind this was that we felt we had enough data to know that it was very unlikely that any of them would result in a viable pregnancy. These embryos were day six and day seven embryos, and had less than optimal embryo grades. Day seven embryos rarely result in viable pregnancies (although it's not unheard of). Typically, it takes an embryo five days to reach the blastocyst stage. The fact that these took six to seven days is a strong indication that they weren't viable.

That being said, having had triplets, we could not justify spending $3,500 on a long shot chance that the frozen embryo transfer would be successful, given none of the others were. We felt these embryos were a part of a "bad batch". The frozen embryos were discarded in accordance with ethical standards. We had been paying a quarterly fee to have them in cryo-preserved storage in Nevada for a few years. We also didn't know if they were chromosomally abnormal or not as we didn't have them tested before freezing or transfer. We didn't want to pass those unknowns along to another couple. Had the embryos been normal, we likely would have donated them to a couple in need. In our case, the data in the form of all of our unsuccessful attempts was a strong indication that the embryos were simply not going to result in a viable pregnancy.

Words of Wisdom

Never Give Up

**"When the world says 'Give Up',
Hope whispers 'Try one more time.'"**

-Anonymous

I feel compelled to offer up words of wisdom from someone who's been through the grind and survived it. I know that there is no right way to behave or feel when you find yourself in the midst of this struggle to conceive. Your feelings are your own—you own them. I certainly owned mine. Personally, I was a wide range of emotions: angry, bitter, frustrated, confused, optimistic, motivated, depressed and ultimately encouraged when we changed our approach and definition of success. And no matter the outcome of your journey, it's a badge, whether you like it or not.

If you truly want a baby, you'll be tested in more ways than you're probably comfortable with. Some people do give up, and that's their choice. What this really means, though, is to find *your* path. Know what it means to be on that path; the risks, the time commitments, the emotional investment and subsequent toll—everything. Have optimism but stay grounded in reality. Finding success is a sacrifice and commitment like no other. In our case, it took an emotional and financial toll on us, but I can say with absolute certainty that it was totally worth it. I personally became obsessed with finding a successful outcome, and was willing to do whatever it took to make that happen. All logic went out the window. I stopped worrying about the cost. I was all in, and so was my wife Angelique. I became a zombie of sorts—one that was unfazed by how many ways I had to split my brain emotionally to take on another IVF cycle. Entering a cycle, I hoped for success, but always braced for failure. I became numb to the grind and obsessed over every detail of each cycle. By the time we reached our final IVF cycle, I knew the process inside and out, and was committed to obtaining the results we both dreamed about. After so much failing, we were both ready to succeed.

It's not easy admitting defeat, let alone failing, but when it comes to trying to conceive, the "fight" is picking yourself back up time and time again and finding the strength to continue on. Unfortunately, there's no magic recipe for success with any of this infertility stuff, but it makes sense to explore all options.

What also eventually needs to happen is a healing period. It's tough after a failed IVF cycle to immediately jump back in and try again. There needs to be time to reflect, grieve and recollect one's thoughts. I thought my wife was really done after our fifth unsuccessful attempt—she was at her breaking point and wasn't sure what else she could do. Everything that she was saying sounded like she didn't see the benefit of continuing on when it wasn't working, and therefore it wasn't meant to be. To that I said, "Bullshit."

I didn't want to give up and didn't want her to think that we had to, so I suggested we try a new path and give ourselves new hope before looking at any other options. That's when we settled on the egg donor path. I just didn't want to see her end up with nothing to show for all of her efforts. I didn't have to inject myself with needles filled with hormones, let alone endure countless procedures in search of answers. My job, all things considered, was the easy one in the equation.

People who end up on the trying-to-conceive path and particularly the ones who endure multiple IVF cycles really want to have children and are heavily invested in the outcome. "Giving up" can mean different things to different people, though. I don't mean it to imply adoption—not at all. I offer this up to motivate anyone contemplating giving up to look deep within and ask yourself why you want to have a child. Believe me, I recognize that a couple's decision to continue on sometimes comes with many conditions. For example, there might be a condition that the resulting child has to be a biological child of their own, or it has to happen before the woman turns forty. Sometimes it's even simpler than that—maybe a couple has all of one gender and has their hearts set on a boy or a girl and they don't necessarily have infertility issues.

Pick a Path and Stay on It

We started out on the IVF path with Angelique's own eggs, and then we switched to IVF with her own eggs and a surrogate. We ended up on that particular path because we believed at the time that it wasn't possible for Angelique to carry a pregnancy on her own.

When we were told by our first IVF doctor to pick a path and stay on it, we believe that the doctor mentioned this because he felt that taking a year off like we did, given how egg quality declines after age thirty-five, was potentially detrimental to our progress, given that Angelique was already thirty-eight years old by this time.

Even though that's likely true, she still needed a break—we needed a break. We had forgotten what it was like to just live our lives without all of the pressure. We used the time off to heal and evaluate our options. We decided it was best to switch doctors and give the new doctor a chance to own our case from start to finish and not inherit someone else's work (frozen embryos). We decided that our path needed to include the following key elements:

- A compassionate IVF doctor (Dr. Kolb was wonderful and made Angelique feel like the most important person on the face of the earth during the time he spent with her during their appointments).
- A knowledgeable support team (GSMoms was invaluable in this regard).
- A list of realistic options, given our history with IVF cycles.

Remain Flexible

In the IVF world, sometimes you have to make tough choices about your future. Sometimes it's necessary to change clinics, travel farther than you'd like, or "invest" in seemingly unnecessary diagnostic bloodwork and procedures. Your pride can make you inflexible—remember that. This can cause someone to rule out an option like sperm or egg donation, or even surrogacy. All that does is reduce the list of options and increase the risks. This can take many forms. For example:

- A couple may be hesitant to "graduate" to IVF because of the associated cost.
- The husband, out of pride, may refuse to consider donor sperm.
- The wife may refuse to consider using donor eggs.
- A couple could be unwilling to consider switching doctors. The result might be sinking money into a clinic where the doctor isn't trying anything new to solve the case.

Don't Forget to Grieve

At the conclusion of our second IVF cycle, we lost a twin pregnancy. I took that loss very hard and it felt like a teeter totter. One of us had to be up so that the other person could be down, and I was very down. I was unable to skip over any of the stages of grief, and I stayed down for a long time, which ultimately forced my wife to stay up and put her own grieving process on hold.

Know What You Can and Can't Handle

Not everyone's cut out for the emotional toll that multiple IVF cycles can take on the body, mind and spirit. As a woman, it's no fun having a cycle fail and even worse to have to deal with your partner's emotions on top of that. How can you not feel that a tremendous weight is on your shoulders? At some point couples realize that it really is out of their hands—it's either going to work or it's not. Unfortunately, IVF provides micro-level insights into what's happening at various stages, yet you're left wondering, after an embryo transfer, if it's going to work or not.

Each loss takes an emotional toll—that much is clear. Once it becomes an obsession, the feelings surrounding a loss become more pronounced, and it's easier to slip into a state of depression and participate in a destructive thinking process. Even before IVF, there's the Clomid cycles, and going through that repeatedly is rough because the side effects tend to get more pronounced as the drug builds up in a woman's system. I remember Angelique getting moodier and moodier with each Clomid cycle, to where it started to impact her job and she decided to switch to taking it at night to "sleep through" the moodiness. Also, as with any drug, the body builds up a tolerance to it.

But it's not just a couple not knowing whether or not they can continue on. Each loss causes one to reflect on specific things such as how certain types of news are delivered, like blood test results or home pregnancy tests.

Couples may ask themselves, "Can I take the call from the nurse or read the email from the doctor?" It's like having a leg or foot injury and the body compensating for that injury. The pregnancy losses or illusive positive results are the injury and couples find themselves questioning their ability to brace themselves for certain kinds of news, so they think of other ways to receive the news.

A Passage of Deep Reflection

There are many things about the journey that led to us becoming parents that I'm not sure I'll ever understand. I've stopped to think about it often, too. Angelique and I endured a lot over the course of seven and a half years, and our surviving it and our eventual reward(s) can be attributed to many things.

It starts with never giving up. Of course, those feelings of hopelessness overwhelmed us as the pregnancy losses mounted, but eventually you become somewhat numb to any feeling of anticipation and go into autopilot in various aspects of your life in order to carry on and ultimately lose yourself in the web of infertility. This might not make any sense, but when I've looked back on the early years, that's exactly what we were both doing. We redirected all of our energy towards making a baby. Nothing else mattered. How did that happen? It's amazing how consumed one can become with trying to conceive. Work becomes a means to an end, seeing babies or pregnant women quickly becomes an unpleasant event, and sex—yes, sex—becomes work and is generally no longer fun because the pressure is on to deliver the goods (for a man) and release that magical egg (for a woman).

One thing I know is that deciding to continue on takes a great deal of strength, and that strength comes and goes. Angelique and I traded places being up and down. Early on, while devastated over a pregnancy loss, she was able to pick herself up and remain positive, while I was not. I was crushed, defeated and confused. I had not been accustomed to failing. Why was this happening to us? As the years went on, Angelique became discouraged and feared the consequences of continuing on and not succeeding. It became so frustrating that mentally she was checked out and going through the motions of fertility treatments, having mastered not getting her hopes up. Once I recognized this, I knew that we had to change our outlook on what success was and this is what ended up being the best path for us. There had to be a path with the balance we so desperately needed.

I took on everything—all Angelique had to do was show up to appointments and "try" to remain calm and relaxed leading up to the embryo transfers. I managed the details of the IVF cycles like when to take medications and when to show up for appointments, dealt with the doctors, handled the financial aspects of each cycle, managed the cycle calendars, and protected my wife from as much bad news as I possibly could.

As exhausting as that was, it was critical. We had been in the game a long time by the time we limped to our final (for financial reasons) IVF cycle. I had acquired more knowledge about infertility and what was going on throughout the entire process than I could have ever imagined, but it was all a product of this obsessive quest for success. There were so many milestones we'd dreamed about in a pregnancy, but never got close to achieving before we chose a different path. All of the medications Angelique had to take to stimulate multiple egg growth had numerous side effects. Each egg retrieval required her to take intravenous antibiotics after the retrieval procedure, and this wiped out her immune system each time. This resulted in her getting colds easily.

Once upon a job, I had an unsupportive boss who, when I told them about our efforts to conceive, asked me how I could put my wife through that knowing the side effects. The polite answer was because I had no choice. When you have to seek the assistance of reproductive technologies, each path requires unique choices with defined outcomes and consequences. It's each person's choice to accept or reject the outcomes and consequences.

In the case of our path, if a woman wants to carry a child and use her own eggs, she must endure injections with often unpredictable side effects, and all with no guarantee that it will work. If a woman or a couple opt out of that, the risk can be shared and a surrogate could carry the pregnancy. If an egg donor is used, there are still injections to prepare the uterus, but the woman (if she gets pregnant) is carrying the child and must endure all that comes with that (that's not easy!).

I knew that, after five unsuccessful cycles, it was extremely important for Angelique to carry a pregnancy, if it was possible. I can't help but look at it as her reward for her sacrifice and commitment to realizing her dream of becoming a mother. I have no idea how she put herself back together for our last cycle—I was sure that she was done, and feared what that could mean for us.

But I knew she was strong and just needed to get on a path with the best chance (given our history) of IVF attempts resulting in a viable pregnancy.

Something strange happened to us once we found out Angelique was pregnant—we expected it to fail, and couldn't figure out why it was continuing on without any of the issues we were used to happening at certain points in the process. Perhaps this was our acquired way of coping. Hopes were so low that we didn't know what to do or how to behave when there was legitimate cause for hope.

I reflect on the serious talks we had with one another when it was clear that we were not only running out of time, money and patience, but emotional energy. They were not easy talks to have, trust me. The analyst/manager in me looked at the situation as objectively as possible and came up with a list of what I felt the options were. It included many things (I won't list them all out), but they were a window into the reality that we weren't exactly on the same page about what could happen and what the options were. I was keenly aware that this experience, much like my father passing away, had changed me—how could it not? The emotional grind of trying to balance my hopes with the true statistics and odds of finding success that were always in play had become a constant and leading worry of mine. Let's keep it in perspective—many couples have split up over infertility, and for many different reasons. As a man, the desire to have children is just as primal as it is for a woman. I can see now why it's easy for some people to take having children for granted.

People wonder how Angelique and I endured all of this heartache, but there were stretches where we both felt like it wasn't

A PASSAGE OF DEEP REFLECTION

going to be possible for us. I remember we were invited to a church and we went there and when it was time to pray, Angelique just broke down and cried, as she was asking God for a baby and didn't understand why it was so hard. I comforted her, but deep down I wondered the same thing. We had so many people praying for us over the years. Back then, we were hoping that the "ask and you shall receive" cliché would work for us. Eventually, we both knew what we had to do in order to protect ourselves, should we decide to continue.

Angelique disconnected from Facebook, declined any and every baby shower invitation, and also steered clear as much as possible from conversations about children. Seeing a baby bump when out around town was probably the most painful trigger for her. Female readers of this book familiar with the "struggle" have probably also glared at a glowing, but complete stranger with a baby bump and whispered to themselves, "Bitch!" Anger is a natural emotion we're confronted with when someone else has something we desperately want.

People who have struggled for years with infertility and end up trying multiple paths out are judged and criticized for their dedication to their cause. One of the toughest judgments is when a couple (or one half of the equation) decides that there is only one path for them. For example, the man or woman determines that it *must* be their biological child. That's any person's right, though. For a woman, that position can have devastating consequences, since there's a time factor in play in terms of egg quality, and it really does depend on the nature of the issue that's preventing a viable pregnancy.

That was our original position, but we ended up compromising, and it was a very fair compromise, especially considering we weren't certain Angelique could carry a pregnancy at all. Angelique's position on having a biological connection changed after seeing a presentation we attended in Pasadena given by the Dr. Kolb, who helped us find success. That slide showed the success rate with donor eggs, and it was consistently higher, regardless of the woman's age. That was very attractive and exactly what Angelique needed. That had to have made it easier to accept for her.

I was willing to compromise because I wanted her to experience pregnancy and I really only had one condition associated with using an egg donor—we both had to come to the conclusion that this person was special. Ideally, we hoped to find someone we both felt connected to and could relate to. I have no idea how we ended up being so lucky with the donor we had, but someone was looking out for us big time.

I didn't touch on donor sperm much thus far in the book, but that is another form of compromise on the man's side. Sometimes there's a male infertility factor that cannot be overcome, and a man must process a sense of loss. Hundreds of millions of sperm are released in an ejaculation, so there's pride in play, as that's a whole lot of opportunities for success. I don't know how you thank someone for that, honestly. We were blessed with three babies—all at once. All healthy and thriving, and all unique and loved to pieces by so many.

Now, though, each day is a triple blessing. We couldn't imagine not having all three babies in our lives. They bring us so much joy and remind us just how precious life is. Gifts that were made possible due to the efforts of a selfless egg donor with a big heart and a passion for helping others and the perfect carrier of these miracles—my wife. What a team they made throughout this process! It all happened so fast after we chose our donor (actually it was a no-brainer). That was an interesting time for all involved. We had two women embarking on IVF cycles for completely different reasons, and we ended up with completely different outcomes. Knowing that our donor was going through her IVF cycle at the same time as us and it was her first, we ended up serving as mentors given we were the veterans in the equation.

One thing that was known, but not openly discussed, was that the cycle could fail for either of us. It would have been particularly devastating for us, but the potential for unpredictable feelings surrounding a loss for either party were high. We had connected with our donor and vice versa. How would one party support the other if it didn't work out? What could the successful party possibly say? It was something that if asked, you could say what you would do or how you would feel, but not with any degree of certainty. We didn't want our donor to experience even a fraction of what we did, but it happened. It wasn't up to us. Same path (IVF), different factors. When it didn't work out for her with her IVF cycle that she did at the same time as Angelique, having split her donated eggs with her, I was upset about it. I didn't think it was fair that someone who had given such a beautiful gift to so many couples should have to experience a loss like we had.

I remember hanging out with the donor's husband in downtown Pasadena. We went out for a long walk to the Rose Bowl and around town before finding a place to sit down and chat over a pitcher of Sangria. He had a great attitude about their journey and what led them to do IVF. Essentially, it was out of his control, and it is what it is, but there was plenty of reason to be optimistic. The reality of the situation was that they were both just as ready as we were to be parents. The irony for our donor was that she was in the infertility industry and used to being on the other side of the table.

The struggle is real, and the triggers are a nuisance when encountered. What I've shared in this chapter is what makes our story so special. You would never imagine an intended parent and a donor actually hitting it off and developing a special bond beyond the cycle itself. Even stranger is my interactions with the donor, where we managed the cycle together, talked all the time, and nobody thought anything of it because it was what needed to be done and it worked.

I often wondered how the donor was able to separate the various emotions, especially after the babies were born. Seeing so many pictures—it takes a special person, truly. But if I'm going to guess, it's easier when you know the babies you helped create are in a nurturing supportive environment with parents who love them to pieces. It's no different than changing a life by donating an organ. We really appreciate her efforts. Our happiness was always her primary concern and her commitment to helping solve our case was extremely important to us. If egg donation were illegal as a general practice and option, so many lives would be impacted, and so many people would not have the chance to realize their dream of being parents.

This path allowed my wife to believe in herself again, and in a way, heal. The emotional scars were deep—I know this because talking about certain aspects of our unique journey with her almost instantly gets the tears flowing, because if you close your eyes you're right back there. That's how it is for us both. You move on with your life, but you never forget. You can't, and you shouldn't. Your experiences make you who you are. We believe these experiences will make us better parents and more understanding when it comes to couples that may be silently struggling. We've been there, done that and know firsthand it's not a pleasant experience to endure. We are thankful there are options available for couples to choose from.

The Helpless Husband

When it comes to having kids, your ability to bear children is something you feel you should have complete control over. It really makes no difference whether you're the male or female in the equation. When I was younger and single, having children wasn't that much of a priority. I felt that I had all the time in the world, and assumed that it would just happen if it was something that I wanted to accomplish when I was ready.

When my wife, Angelique, and I got married, having a child together became a near-term goal. At that point we both probably still felt that we could control when it would happen and that there would be no issues along the way. In fact, we weren't even thinking that there would be issues—we knew NOTHING of the dark period that represents an infertility struggle. After my father passed away in 2008, having children of my own became increasingly important. The desire to have a piece of me carry on in this world after I am gone became a strong desire and, ultimately, a mission—

one where failure was not an option. I will walk through the various phases we went through during our journey to our three miracles in detail, and it will show how increasingly helpless I felt as a husband.

Trying the Natural Way

Less than one year after getting married, Angelique and I had moved back to Sacramento and made the decision to start trying the old-fashioned (natural) way: she ovulates, we have sex in the days before and after ovulation, wait a few weeks before she takes a home pregnancy test. She had been off birth control for over a year by this time. She was regularly charting her basal body temperature, monitoring her cervical mucus, everything someone monitoring specific signs in order to time things right for conception would do. She even bought ovulation predictor kits, but soon found that they would never have a positive line. Her cycles were really long—on average, north of forty-five days. Her method of telling me she wasn't pregnant was finding me and just telling me, "I started."

I would simply say, "Oh, ok.", and we would continue on with the rest of our days.

Months went by with this news, and it started to get very frustrating to hear. I would ask myself, "Is it me that's the issue? Is there something that I can do?" My job was pretty simple in the equation: deliver the sperm. The rest was out of my hands. I still tried to do more, though. I wanted to be more helpful.

I love using technology to make things easier, and started charting her cycle in spreadsheets and looking for a pattern or trend. As the months continued to accumulate, the spreadsheets became more detailed. The level of detail started to make me believe we were getting a better sense for when she would actually ovulate. She made one change in her diet by starting a fruit and vegetable juicing regimen, and that caused her to have positive ovulation tests for the first time ever.

But then there would be an anomaly. For example, in one cycle that we were tracking, she went seventy days without a period. Tracking then shifted to demoralizing, and I started to realize that this was truly out of my control. At that point we decided to seek help from a doctor.

"Graduating" to Working with a Doctor

We arrived at Kaiser Permanente hospital in Roseville, California for our first appointment, which was actually a workshop with other couples also trying to conceive. We were handed presentation materials. The room was packed with couples. I saw couples that appeared to be newlyweds, but also couples that just had this look like they had been trying for a while. Some of the husbands looked ashamed to be there, while others looked disinterested, as if they didn't want to be there supporting their wives at all. These husbands had the "This is beneath me" look on their faces.

We sat in the front of the conference room and the presentation was actually pretty boring because we had acquired a lot of knowledge doing our own research during our attempts to conceive. Still, before the break we realized that Kaiser's first step was to have couples start from scratch, which involved getting back to basics: a calendar, knowing when the woman's last menstrual period was, and timing sex around the time the woman ovulates. At the break, the instructor took questions, and this was a defining moment in our struggle to conceive. Angelique flagged down the instructor and essentially poured out her frustrations to the woman and broke down and cried. She told her how badly she wanted a baby and how she didn't know why it wasn't working or what else she could do. She told the woman that she was thirty-four years old and felt she was running out of time. I stood there, for the first time feeling helpless, as I wasn't expecting that to happen. The woman listened, looked Angelique in the eyes while holding her firmly by the shoulders, and said, "We're going to get you pregnant, my dear."

She was right (eventually), but for different reasons. The instructor saying that to Angelique gave her hope when her spirits were already down, having not found success on her own. I felt helpless in that I didn't know if I could even understand how Angelique must have been feeling—the pressure she was putting on herself to make this happen, the sense of pride that fueled her quest to get pregnant on her own without needing any medical assistance and the resulting stress was something I don't think I was prepared to understand.

What could I possibly do to make her feel like her body wasn't letting her down? I didn't have that answer at this stage and wasn't prepared to acknowledge any of the possible options and their associated risks and costs. I was just trying to keep my own spirits up and exercise as much patience as I possibly could, but this phase soon proved to be just as frustrating because I really didn't think we were working towards anything.

We both agreed that the initial steps Kaiser Permanente hospital recommended were not going to work for us, and that we needed to escalate our efforts. We began working with an infertility doctor through Kaiser Permanente at this point. This produced an immediate rush of excitement for both of us, and I personally didn't feel so helpless anymore.

Clomid Cycles

I best can sum up the Clomid cycles that Angelique did with one word: Scary. Clomid is a pill prescribed by IVF doctors which causes a woman's eggs to mature faster and in greater quantities. The doctor does vaginal ultrasounds every few days for a few weeks to monitor follicle growth. Usually there are one or two really dominant follicles at the conclusion of the medication cycle. Doctors then "trigger" ovulation with a hormone shot called Human Chorionic Gonadotropin (HCG). The Clomid cycles were scary because the medication changed Angelique's personality. She first started taking it in the mornings, which was catastrophic because it made her extremely moody at work.

Angelique was a very bubbly and chipper person, and she was well known at her job for her happy personality. She got into an argument with some woman at work and got a talking to by management as a result. They recognized that this behavior was very uncharacteristic of Angelique. After that happened, we made the decision to have her take the medication at night, so she could (we hoped) sleep through the side effects. This made a huge difference.

The Clomid cycles were somewhat exciting in that we had routine ultrasounds to check the growth of the follicles, which gave us an opportunity to see positive progress. The doctor would measure them all, and it was great to see the measurement numbers go up. The unfortunate reality with Clomid is that there's a short window with the drug where it is not effective after six cycles or so.

Things turned frustrating after we reached the point where we were going to the doctor for the trigger shot injection, and days later Angelique's period would arrive. You can imagine how she must have felt with her hormones already on edge due to the medication and then having to process the news that the cycle was not successful.

What more can I do?" became a core question that I asked myself over and over again. How else could I help her? Why wasn't this working? Another frustrating "side effect" for Angelique with the Clomid approach was what we saw after each "check-in" ultrasound prior to starting a new cycle. The ultrasound would reveal that her follicles had turned into cysts, which forced us to skip a cycle and hope that the cysts went away. The doctor usually put her back on birth control. We didn't know what was causing this—it could have been that the HGC hormone injection didn't produce a surge that was strong enough to cause the egg to release from the follicle, which resulted in the cysts.

Eventually Angelique expressed concern with this Clomid path and asked the doctor to advance us to the next step in the process, which resulted in another doctor and even more medication. The next phase for us was Clomid plus Menopur and IUI.

Intra Uterine Insemination (IUI) Attempts

The Clomid and IUI cycles were the most physically taxing attempts for Angelique to date. She had to deal with the side effects from the Clomid and its dosage being increased, and then turn around and do needle injections with Menopur, a medication which burns going in.

I'll never forget the first IUI cycle we did. I had to give a semen sample, which was washed and prepared to be artificially inseminated into Angelique through her cervix. As she laid on the table waiting for the vial to come back, we talked about how exciting it was.

Then the nurse (go figure, the same woman who at the Kaiser Permanente infertility seminar gave the presentation and consoled Angelique at the break when she broke down and cried) opened the door with a tray that had a vial on it labeled with Angelique's medical record number. I swear that all sounds in the room went silent once I saw that vial on the tray. I realized that was a piece of me in that vial and it had the capability of producing a life. The nurse sees so many patients that she had long forgotten us from the seminar. She inserted the sperm into Angelique's cervix and told her to lay there for thirty minutes. She returned later to tell us to go home and have fun doing the baby dance for the next three days. We happily obliged.

Unfortunately, Angelique's period came about a week later and we were left wondering what to do next. The second IUI attempt was cancelled because the doctor determined after the final ultrasound before administering the trigger shot that Angelique's ovaries had responded too well to the medication. She had eighteen mature follicles that could have released and been fertilized. The doctor advised us not to proceed and we accepted his recommendation. At this point, the doctor's advice actually instilled fear in us about the possibility and risk of having high order multiples. It was disappointing, but we agreed it wasn't worth rolling the dice and ignoring the doctor's advice and ending up with her as the next Octomom.

The Clomid and IUI cycles were interesting because the doctor would adjust the dosages of both the Clomid and the Menopur based on what he saw as far as follicle growth on the ultrasound. At one point the dosages were so high that Angelique could feel that they were growing rapidly. I can see why couples that find success with this option usually end up with high-order multiples (triplets, quads or quintuplets).

By the time we reached this path, I had these burning questions: Why wasn't this working for us? What was keeping it from working? What could I do to make it work? Clearly, as these were my questions as a husband, I felt that I could influence the outcome. The reality was that we were at the mercy of the doctors and the stars aligning.

IVF #1 (Fresh Cycle)

Our first fresh IVF cycle was an emotional roller coaster. The IVF doctor retrieved twenty-eight eggs from Angelique after weeks of injections and we ended up with several embryos. We felt as if we had more control of our destiny as a result. The IVF doctor gave us the option (spun as an "incentive") of transferring a single embryo into Angelique's uterus since it was our first ever IVF cycle, and if it didn't work, the first frozen embryo transfer would essentially be free (less the costs associated with preparing her uterus for the frozen embryo transfer). This is usually offered by IVF doctors as a strategy to reduce the chances of multiple births (twins, triplets or higher).

We wanted to give ourselves the best odds, so we elected to transfer two embryos. We waited about a week before the first blood test, but after Angelique got her blood drawn at the lab to test for the presence of the pregnancy hormone we received a call from one of the IVF nurses that her HCG level was thirty-six and that she was pregnant. We were over the moon with joy! It wasn't a strong number out the gate, but the rule of thumb was that the HCG level should at least double every forty-eight hours. Angelique was excited because she had been peeing on a stick and the results were coming back negative, and this caused her to become depressed about the outcome.

Two days later we went in for a blood test, and the HCG number was fifty-eight. The nurse who called with that news called Angelique directly and she was at work. The nurse was very blunt and told Angelique to prepare for the worst. Angelique called me sobbing and I left work immediately to go comfort her. I found her outside of the building crying next to a tree. I held her tight and asked what the nurse said. After she explained to me how blunt and pessimistic the nurse had been, I called the doctor and requested that all news be directed my way moving forward, and that I would be the one to inform my wife.

The next few blood tests revealed that the HCG levels were not rising like the doctor expected. By the time we got to the six-week ultrasound, the doctor performed an ultrasound and saw a gestational yolk sac, but with no fetal pole. I can best describe it as a hot air balloon rising into the sky, but with no passenger.

The official diagnosis was a blighted ovum and therefore a biochemical pregnancy. The doctor called in another doctor (the doctor we had worked with during the early Clomid cycles before graduating to IUI and IVF), and he also looked at the ultrasound and confirmed our doctor's assessment. The IVF doctor recommended that she receive an injection to expel the failed pregnancy rather than wait for her to miscarry. We took his advice and scheduled the next step.

Unfortunately, the same nurse who was so cold and pessimistic over the phone greeted us in the waiting area and asked us to come back with her—she informed us that she would be administering the shot. She reached out to give Angelique a hug and asked, "How are you doing?"

Angelique just gave her this, "How do you think?" look and reluctantly hugged her back. She said hello to me, but I was upset so I just pretended to read emails on my Blackberry. She administered the shot for Angelique and told us to have a nice day. I understand that the medical staff do this all day long and it benefits them to leave the emotional component out of their work seeing so many patients throughout the day, but we were both hurting from the loss and could have used some compassion during that ordeal. I personally felt helpless in that I couldn't stop my wife's pain. We wanted out of that hospital so badly after the procedure.

Needless to say, it was a very quiet ride home. "There's always next time" was something I dared not say anytime soon—Angelique needed time to grieve and process the loss. Given this was our first loss after having received confirmation that she was actually pregnant, neither of us really knew how to deal with our feelings. It didn't really matter how much money we had spent on this attempt. It was a tough pill to swallow watching our hopes for this cycle vanish. I felt I had to watch my wife's excitement fade before my eyes. She was physically and emotionally exhausted from this cycle.

Her body didn't recover well from the egg procedure itself. She was physically miserable in the days after the embryo transfer because she was experiencing mild Ovarian Hyper Stimulation Syndrome symptoms, which included severe abdominal bloating and pain, tenderness in her ovaries and sudden weight gain.

IVF #2 (1st Frozen Cycle)

After the devastating loss with our first IVF attempt, Angelique showed incredible strength and determination as we scheduled our first frozen embryo transfer. She was so positive as we initially engaged with the doctor. She told me, "This will be our cycle—I just know it!", and I believed her.

When we got to the clinic for the initial pre-screening ultrasound to ensure it was safe to do a transfer, I remember being excited when we arrived at the IVF clinic as it felt good to be back for another attempt. I felt as if it was OK to have hope this cycle. We had a better sense for what to expect and were more prepared this time to navigate the various twists and turns of each phase of an IVF cycle.

This time Angelique only had to prepare her uterus for an embryo transfer. There was no recovering from an egg retrieval procedure to contend with. I had just started a new job at a new department—_much_ more on that later. I was committed to being there for my wife. I was at every appointment and knew the medication protocol inside and out. I also functioned as the liaison in the equation so that all my wife had to do was show up for her appointments. By this time administering the shots were a piece of cake.

Our outlook on this cycle was extremely positive. For this next cycle, we elected to thaw and transfer two embryos to once again give ourselves decent odds. We accepted the risk that one embryo (or both) could split, resulting in quadruplets. (This does happen, actually.)

The embryos thawed beautifully. The embryologist knocked on the door and brought them out. She said hello to us, and I remember that same feeling I had when the nurse brought the washed and prepared sperm out on that silver tray. This feeling was even stronger than that, and more exciting. In that plastic vial was a genetic union of Angelique and me—it was two embryos with the potential to become babies. They represented two opportunities for us to realize our dreams of having a family.

We watched the ultrasound screen with excitement as the embryos were transferred into Angelique's uterus. We went home one hour later, and the waiting game began. Angelique reported the usual cramping, which could have been a sign of implantation occurring, but there was just this feeling that this was out of my control. There I was again, feeling helpless. It didn't matter how many candles I lit, or what infertility discussion threads I read—every couple's journey and outcome is unique.

Angelique resisted peeing on a stick early on for this particular IVF cycle; however, eventually she gave in and started testing. This is a common obsession for women struggling to conceive. It can become a painful lesson learned, though, and ultimately an additional source of stress.

One day she sent me a photo from her phone of a positive pregnancy test. I was at work and in a meeting but after reading her text message I let out a "Holy shit!!!" and left the meeting. She was surprised because she had been testing negative and spotting, so she was worried that the IVF cycle might be failing.

The first blood test came back a few days later with an HCG level of seventy-nine. The nurse who called this time was very positive and congratulated me. I passed the news along to Angelique over the phone and she was very excited. I ran through the building at work and located my boss's office. My boss just happened to be in a one-on-one meeting with another staff. I poked my head in and gave two thumbs up and ran off. She had this look on her face like, "Why is he so excited and why did he just burst in here like that?". She wasn't too familiar (let alone concerned) with my story or struggles to start a family—she just didn't get it. Despite that, I was so excited I didn't know what to do with myself. When I got home, Angelique and I shared a long hug and she cried. Angelique said, "I told you this was our cycle!", and I smiled. We were on our way.

The second blood test revealed an HCG level of 279, which had more than doubled. Angelique was elated! The nurse who called me said that things were looking very good and to have her do another blood test in two days. That HCG level came back in the 900 range, and at that point we knew we had a strong pregnancy. The next blood test a week later came back in the 4,000 range, and we suspected that both embryos may have taken and that we might be expecting twins. The six-week ultrasound confirmed this. The doctor saw two yolk sacs and fetal poles. We were blown away. I could see Angelique believing in herself again and starting to relax—somewhat.

We would soon discover that there is no relaxing that early into an IVF cycle. Angelique was in the kitchen with her mom baking, when she felt something rupture. She went to the bathroom and blood was gushing into the toilet. She felt that something was wrong. As she sat on the toilet, she said, "I'm so sorry, honey...".

I was just outside the bathroom, and didn't know what to say. I called Kaiser Permanente and told them what was happening, and they told us to come in to see the doctor the next day. I told my boss that I would not be in that day because my wife was pregnant with twins and was experiencing complications. My boss said that she hoped everything was OK. I accompanied Angelique to the ultrasound. The doctor inserted the vaginal ultrasound probe and we saw the two gestational sacs and fetal poles. He pressed a few buttons on the ultrasound machine and blue and red streaks jetted across the screen, exactly like Doppler radar.

"What's that?" I asked.

"Those are the heart beats," he said. We were speechless.

The doctor told us everything looked to be in order and not to worry. Angelique felt relieved, and we went back home feeling we were still in the game. We were in week six with this current IVF cycle attempt. Our previous and very first IVF had cycle failed by the sixth week, and we were told to come back for another ultrasound the following week (seven weeks), as the doctor was not overly concerned about what had transpired at home that caused us to come in for the emergency ultrasound.

When we went for the follow-up ultrasound the following week, we saw that both gestational sacs had collapsed. The pregnancy had failed. We were both devastated. The doctor finished up the ultrasound and left us alone for a while. I broke down and cried—this wasn't what I was expecting to see at all. Angelique was the strong one this day, and she comforted me. I couldn't understand why this was happening. Was all of the bleeding she experienced at six weeks the start of the failing pregnancy? It rocked us both to our core. Where did we go from here?

I emailed my boss the news and she expressed her condolences, but I wasn't myself at all when I went back to work. This was a major loss, and I became depressed. I didn't say much at the office, had trouble concentrating, and regretted taking on a new job in a new organization while trying to start a family by way of a process as emotionally taxing as IVF. I started this new job September 2011 and the IVF cycle failed October 2011. I had no idea the toll that the failures would take on a couple. It was a tall order to take on a new job at a new organization and also attempt to be a supportive husband during an IVF cycle. I was unable to bifurcate my emotions during this time.

What made matters worse was that things weren't going well at that job. It seemed as if my boss took pleasure in kicking me while I was down. I didn't share what I was going through with many people at that organization, but I don't think this boss understood how important this was to me. It's neither here nor there, but it left a bad taste in my mouth, and, as a manager, I made a promise to myself to always be empathetic to my direct reports—you never know what someone's going through or how your reaction to whatever it is will impact their well-being. Empathy goes a long way.

IVF #3 (2nd Frozen Cycle with the First Batch of Embryos)

I ultimately ended up deciding that my family was more important than my career ambitions, and I elected to return to my previous department only four months in to my tenure there. It was an easy decision. I could not stomach that job and the unrealistic expectations while supporting myself emotionally as Angelique also recovered emotionally from the devastating loss of the twin pregnancy.

By January of 2012, I was back at my old department. I wasn't given my old job back—I was to be assigned work based on the department's current needs. There was a new head of IT, and I had the displeasure of learning that this boss was not empathetic either. I was both thrilled and relieved to be back because I knew the work, the people and the organization well, and I could at least function in the job while being there for my wife. I had a low stress job and no direct reports—I was assigned to a special project.

A few months passed, and Angelique and I discussed trying again and decided to proceed with another frozen embryo transfer IVF cycle with Kaiser Permanente in April of 2012. We were excited to be back on the train again. I missed being at the IVF clinic regularly. I also felt that, since we still had some inventory to work with thanks to the frozen embryos, we were still in the game and could find success.

I did notice one thing: When the embryologist would bring us the embryos, there was an embryo grade associated with each embryo on the embryologist's report. I noticed that the embryo grade was changing. I had done some research and knew that they transferred the highest-graded embryos first. The quality of the embryos we were now transferring was declining. For example, there was now fragmentation in play, possibly a result of the freezing process, and it may have impacted these embryos. Also, the number of cells were decreasing. Another concerning factor linked to the chances for a viable pregnancy was how long it took the embryo to develop in the laboratory environment and reach the blastocyst stage of embryo development. Typically, this happens at day five of the embryo development process, but some embryos reach it at day six or seven. The longer it takes to reach it, the greater the concern that the embryo is not viable.

We also faced new challenges by the time we got to embryo transfer day: with frozen embryo transfers, you show up and they thaw the embryos a few hours before. If one doesn't thaw and you have extras, they thaw another one. It's a pretty unnerving period because you don't know when you show up if you have anything to transfer. This time, the doctor came back and told us that one of the two embryos we requested be thawed did not survive the thawing process and that they were thawing another one. The doctor asked us if we wanted it discarded. We asked him if we could just throw it in with the other two as it wasn't helping or hurting matters. Still, it wasn't easy hearing that an embryo did not survive the thawing process.

We started to get a sense for the types of risks couples encounter with IVF, and my helpless feeling took on a whole new meaning. I wasn't expecting to feel helpless for different reasons. We transferred the two embryos and the waiting game began.

This IVF cycle, Angelique elected not to pee on a stick. She didn't want to worry herself any more than absolutely necessary. A little over a week later, we got a call from the doctor that Angelique was pregnant again. She cried and smiled. We knew the drill by this time, and we just waited for the two days to pass before she would go in for another blood test. After she went in for another blood test, the doctor called me back and said that the hormone levels had doubled. We were pleasantly surprised. Unfortunately, the next blood test two days later was shocking. The hormone levels had dropped to zero…ZERO.

I told Angelique the news, and she stormed out of the family room angrily. She went upstairs and slammed the door. She didn't say much for the rest of the evening. I went upstairs, but she didn't want to talk. She just laid on the couch in the upstairs master bedroom and watched TV. She was trying to watch happy movies. It was clear she didn't want to dwell on the loss.

My boss was aware of our latest attempt, and said something interesting to me: "Why do you keep putting your wife through all of this with the injections and medication?"

The answer was simple: it is a product of the path we chose. We didn't have the luxury of trying the old-fashioned way and finding success, saving a bunch of money in the process. I was insulted. It just demonstrated that this person knew nothing of the process and how difficult success was to achieve. I don't think any woman enjoys the needles, the endless medication, the bloated feeling, cramping, or invasive exploratory procedures that are necessary to even do IVF at all.

In addition to the special project I had been assigned to manage, I had also been assigned to manage a new unit at the time of the latest IVF loss. I didn't show how badly I was hurting to any of my staff. A few months after the loss, I accepted a new job at another department (the same department where Angelique worked). I had a personal meeting with two of my staff that I had gotten to know pretty well over the course of the six months being back at my previous department, and shared the story of our infertility journey. They had no idea I was going through any of this. One of them cried at the end of the story. The most interesting comment one of the staff made was that they could not tell that I had endured a devastating loss like this because I carried myself with the utmost professionalism while at work. They said that I must have been an incredibly strong individual. I think that by that point I had learned to separate my emotions about our infertility struggles from work. I needed to be focused on only work while at work. I knew better than to take my personal frustrations out on anyone at work.

The One-Year Break

My wife and I decided after this latest loss that it was time to take a break and regroup. We had no timetable for when we would try again or what the path would be. By this time, Angelique was feeling like a failure, and I wasn't sure what I could do to help her.

Angelique and I had hit the point in our efforts to have a baby where we needed to take a break. It seemed as if we weren't any closer to understanding what the problem was, and we needed to step away from "the grind" that is IVF. This didn't mean that we didn't think about it, though.

So, we took a year off and tried to carry on with our lives despite this empty feeling we had. Fortunately, we had Dinky, who was a dog Angelique's mom had found. Dinky started out with Angelique's mom, but ended up living with us for a while. Angelique fell in love with him when she saw him and really wanted the companionship.

The one-year break was very challenging because of all of the triggers that were still present. Others around us kept having kids, Angelique kept seeing pregnant women everywhere she looked, and people would still tell us to just go on vacation and it would happen for us.

During that year, we were able to talk about the previous losses, but weren't sure how to proceed. We had concerns about the first batch of embryos—the outcome was the same, but we were starting to scrape the bottom of our inventory barrel.

IVF #4 (2nd Fresh Cycle – The Joint Surrogacy Cycle)

This was a very interesting cycle. I can admit that at this point we were getting desperate. Angelique's sister Missy was very familiar with our struggles and offered to be a surrogate for us. At this point, we assumed that there might be something that was preventing Angelique from successfully carrying a pregnancy to term. Missy had two children and had no issues getting or staying pregnant. She was forty-one years old at the time, and in good health. We took her up on her offer, I did a Google search and found a local surrogacy agency (Gestational Surrogate Moms or GSMoms), and we began down the path of surrogacy with our current IVF doctor at Kaiser Permanente hospital.

We had to enter into a surrogacy contract, which spelled out all of the terms that would govern the agreement, and Angelique's sister had to be medically cleared to carry, which she was. We all had to undergo counseling sessions as well.

Once the contract was signed, her sister embarked on the journey that we were already intimately familiar with and she also got a taste of the emotional component that comes with an IVF cycle. All of a sudden, the stakes are high. Her sister was confident that she would get this done for us because her body had never let her down.

We had always transferred two embryos with each IVF cycle to give ourselves the best possible odds. When we approached Angelique's sister about transferring two, she refused. She was confident she could successfully carry one baby to term—two felt too risky for her.

Angelique and I weren't expecting this. We had to respect her choice, but this caused Angelique and I to re-evaluate our approach. Angelique had already gotten used to the idea of giving her body a break, as she wouldn't have to turn around after an egg retrieval and prepare her body to receive an embryo. That changed with her sister's decision, so she threw her name (and body) back into the equation and signed up to also have two embryos transferred to her own uterus.

As you read this, you may be thinking, "He convinced two women to carry his child at the same time. What a stud!" All jokes aside, it was all about the odds of success, and we took the option that was available to have two parallel paths that could lead to a child or children.

Here's what happened: Angelique went through the egg retrieval procedure while her sister was preparing her uterus via the injections, progesterone and subsequent monitoring. The twenty-four eggs that were retrieved were fertilized. Her sister Missy had one embryo transferred, as per the contractual agreement, while Angelique had two embryos transferred.

Then the waiting game started, times two. When it came time to get the blood test results, I received the call directly about both results from the nurse. Angelique's sister Missy's pregnancy test came back with a positive result but a low HCG level of twenty-four—but she was pregnant. Angelique's result came back with an HCG level of five, which was not considered pregnant and therefore unsuccessful.

Angelique's reaction was not extreme. It was like she had already prepared for the worst and wasn't surprised with the result. I called her sister with the results and she was shocked. She commented that she didn't feel pregnant, which I think was fueled by the fact that she wasn't used to having these types of insights offered up. With her pregnancies, I don't think she got any blood work done, and most certainly wasn't provided any HCG levels. This created a wave of anticipation about the next blood test and what the HCG level would be.

I told her that doctors like to see the next HGC level at least double every forty-eight hours. She was still confident after hearing that, but once the second blood test results revealed that the HCG level only went up a few points, she was shocked. This was an indication that the pregnancy was failing. She became sad and apologized for letting us down. We didn't feel like she had let us down. She was confused, as she had never had any issues staying pregnant. I explained to her that there must have been something wrong with the embryo that was transferred and that it was nothing that she did.

Still, I believe after this outcome, she became humbled and began to empathize with her sister's pain, and also realized that this was something that was out of her hands as well. A surrogate is a vehicle, but not the deciding factor. So many things have to align (a healthy embryo, the right embryo conditions, etc.). It just didn't work out. At this point, Angelique and I began to worry that there might be an egg quality issue, and we needed to evaluate what our next move would be.

IVF #5 (3rd Fresh Cycle - New IVF Doctor)

By the time we reached IVF cycle attempt #5, I had reached the point where I was wondering what more I could do to help us achieve a successful outcome. After both pregnancies failed with the surrogacy cycle, we briefly discussed the outcome with the IVF doctor at Kaiser. At this point he was emotionally invested in our case as well. He didn't say much other than for us to try again, but we could tell he wasn't happy about the outcome; like he too had been robbed of an opportunity to succeed.

We also discussed the outcome with our surrogacy coordinator Lisa at GSMoms, and she suggested that we consider switching doctors. She put us in contact again with Dr. Bradford Kolb from Huntington Reproductive Center in Pasadena, California.

As mentioned previously, we ended up switching to Dr. Kolb and trying one more time with Angelique's own eggs. Dr. Kolb had a different protocol that he followed for trigger shots. Instead of Ovidrel, he used a Lupron trigger. The difference with Angelique was that she recovered quickly, was on her feet the next day and wasn't overstimulated.

Unfortunately, Doctor Kolb's egg retrieval only yielded four viable eggs, which was a significantly lower total than all of Angelique's previous egg retrievals. She was thirty-eight years old and had already had an egg retrieval earlier in the year that yielded twenty-four eggs. What had changed? Was her ovarian reserve depleting that fast? In any event, it was a sign that nature's law of diminishing returns that governs egg quality after age thirty-five was at work.

We transferred two embryos, and while the pregnancy test

was initially positive, the next HCG level was zero. This result essentially told us we were done attempting to use Angelique's eggs. I had secured the services of one of the best IVF doctors around, and we still weren't able to find success, so naturally I was wondering what else I could do. It just didn't work, and by this point I felt like a spectator, unable to influence the outcome in any way whatsoever.

IVF #6 (Donor Egg Cycle)

I will humbly acknowledge that by the time Angelique and I reached what would be our final IVF cycle involving the use of donor eggs, we both had very little (emotionally) in the tank. I realized that I had done pretty much all I could do, and that if this was going to be successful, there wasn't much else I could do except remain positive. We were on the brink of financial collapse, and when the opportunity to be matched with an experienced egg donor emerged, it gave us a renewed sense of hope.

By the time this option had emerged, Angelique knew that she was done attempting to use her own eggs—she just wanted a healthy baby. She didn't even care if the donor didn't look like her—if the donor's eggs were good, that was good enough for her! She still had that presentation slide from Dr. Kolb's free infertility seminar burned into her mind. With the egg donor path, the chances of success were consistently higher, despite the woman's age.

As we embarked on this cycle with our donor, Angelique was mostly silent. I don't think she knew what to expect. I believe she had reached the point where she was indifferent about the outcome.

Her role with the final cycle was different. She was no longer expected to grow eggs and then turn around and prepare her uterus to receive the resulting embryos—the donor was taking on the burden of the egg production. She was more relaxed during the egg stimulation and retrieval portion of the IVF cycle. I remember her commenting a few times that it was so nice to not have to put her body through that—she could relax for a bit. Little did we know she would need to save her strength for what was behind "Door Number Three".

Our donor, Kayla was so helpful leading up to and during our IVF cycle. Her being a veteran egg donor as well as the director of the egg donor arm of the surrogacy agency that we had previously worked with gave us a resource with incredible knowledge and experience in multiple sectors of the infertility industry. We both had very high confidence in Kayla and Dr. Kolb, as they were both results-oriented individuals with a track record for producing successful results. Once the IVF cycle got going, we had no choice but to put our faith in those two doing their jobs and left the outcome to God. The time had come to trust the process.

We had wagered everything we had on our last best chance at having kids. This last IVF cycle was the defining moment in our journey to becoming parents. Every investment was an attempt to influence an outcome, not necessarily control it. Each unsuccessful attempt increased our frustrations, and personally caused me to feel that much more helpless. I wanted so badly for Angelique to not have to go through any of these infertility struggles, but my best efforts to support her by taking on so much each cycle did not change the fact that there was only so much that I could do to make our dream a reality before it was out of my hands.

The Number of Embryos to Transfer—A Difficult Decision

In the early days of IVF, there were very few limits placed on the number of embryos to transfer. Then again, the success rate wasn't as high as it is today. Advancements in technology have resulted in improved odds of a live birth, and with more embryos sticking and resulting in live births, the odds of having multiples went up as well. When we first started on our IVF journey, new guidelines were in place. Our fertility clinic had an "incentive program", as they called it. They encouraged couples going through their first IVF cycle to transfer only a single embryo. The incentive was that if the cycle wasn't successful, the first frozen embryo transfer would be "free". The goal was to limit the chances of multiples. Of course, a single embryo could still split into twins, but more and more couples were finding success transferring more than one embryo and were ending up with twins, triplets or other high-order multiples.

For our first IVF cycle, we were presented with the incentive program, but declined because we were already veterans well into our infertility journey and IVF was a graduation of sorts for us, where the stakes were higher, and we were investing in a "higher percentage shot". Our plan was to transfer two embryos at a time to increase our chances of success, and that's exactly what we did. What's funny is that at one point we asked our first IVF doctor about his thoughts on transferring three embryos. He advised against it, and I believe his exact words were, "Triplets would be a nightmare!"

Actually, one early cycle we had transferred three embryos; however, it wasn't really three as the third one was a thawed embryo that didn't score quite high enough. We just threw it in for sentimental reasons knowing it likely wouldn't result in a baby.

Our last cycle, we had transferred four embryos. It was everything we had from our donor cycle and we knew that it was our last best chance. So technically, had all four taken (who knows, maybe they all did initially), we could have ended up with quads. The thing about that decision is that it could have ended differently and not with a positive outcome. For example, we could have lost more than one of the babies over the course of the pregnancy (or all of them depending on complications and when they arrived).

Now that Michaela, Emma and Christopher are here with us, we talk about what it would be like to have two Michaela babies, or two Christopher babies. Their personalities are a lot to handle as they are growing up, but as babies they were both very demanding in different ways. That would be crazy! Emma wasn't as demanding as her siblings as a baby, so that helped.

But our decision to transfer all of our embryos resulted in very favorable odds. One of the things we talked about when we settled on the number four was whether or not we were really ready for the challenges this would entail if successful. I believe that not every parent is equipped to be a parent of multiples, but we just happened to be.

Sure, our lives would have been easier had we decided to transfer just one embryo. We would have had a singleton baby to contend with, and maybe it would have still been Michaela. But would Angelique still have had the mental energy (and would we have had the financial capacity) to go back for two subsequent cycles to arrive at the two other babies that currently make up our family? That is doubtful, and scary to think about as our family feels like it was meant to contain each one of our children. Obviously, we had three perfectly good embryos that resulted in live births, and we are honored with the choice we made to proceed with all three. Still, other couples make different, difficult decisions, such as embryo storage and embryo donation or destruction. None of these are easy choices. Embryo storage has a long-term financial impact, embryo donation a biological impact (can a couple accept that they have another biological child out there?) and embryo destruction comes with ethical concerns, especially if the embryos are of a high quality.

The health risks are also something that should be factored into the decision. Doctors typically don't allow couples to transfer more than two embryos. Our case was unique in that we had so many previous attempts. Carrying high-order multiples carries significant risks to both the mother and the babies. The woman isn't guaranteed to make it all the way to her delivery date, and with each week the baby is born early, the list of health issues to overcome lengthens. Doctors attempt to prepare couples for the NICU experience, but it's unique to each couple and the emotional grind wears on a person the longer their child stays in the NICU. Some couples lose a child before ever bringing them home or in some cases shortly thereafter. In some of the most unfavorable circumstances, the children can end up with severe disabilities and/or developmental delays. We were lucky that our children's health issues were all relatively minor.

The Financial Toll

It might appear that the most humbling portion of our journey was not being in control of our fertility, but I've come to realize that it's actually the financial toll that the desire and quest to have children can create.

When Angelique and I were childless, we were a great team. Financially, I took care of the macro (visionary) financial transactions such as finding the house, the cars, investing in solar and saving for the future. I took an assortment of different credit risks in order to make this happen. Angelique was largely focused on the micro (operational) details of our union. She managed the grocery budget, furnished our home and financially supported our lifestyle in other "micro" ways.

We had a great life. We had a beautiful, five-bedroom, three-bathroom home in Antelope, California. We both worked in government jobs for the state and had very good incomes. We also both had excellent credit. This turned out to be a blessing and a curse.

We often joined "credit forces" on purchases such as automobiles. Her credit score was a little higher than mine, as she took different risks than I did. In those early years of our relationship and marriage, we would accumulate "smart debt", refinance it into lower interest credit cards, and eventually pay cards and loans off. When our infertility journey started, we weren't worried about loans so much. We had comfortable nest eggs set aside in savings thanks to placing the equity from selling previous homes into savings.

But all of that started to change as the struggles began to accumulate. Our savings accounts got lower and lower, and, by the time we "graduated" to IVF, we turned to credit.

I remember financing the first major cycle with Kaiser Permanente hospital using a personal loan. I viewed the payment as an investment in our future, and fully expected that we would only need at most two IVF cycles in order to be successful. Boy, was I ever wrong. After the first fresh IVF cycle ($12,000) failed, we were ready to pursue a frozen embryo transfer IVF cycle. There was a cost associated with this of about $2,500. That cost didn't include whatever medications Angelique needed in order to prepare her uterus to receive the thawed embryo(s). We had several credit cards, but this first cycle we paid for with money from savings, further depleting our reserves.

Kaiser Permanente hospital stored frozen embryos on site in Sacramento for the first six months, but after six months the embryos were shipped to a cryo-storage facility in Reno, Nevada, and a quarterly fee of $106 was charged.

The first frozen embryo transfer was unsuccessful, and we started to incur that quarterly embryo storage fee. The next few frozen embryo transfer attempts with Kaiser Permanente were financed via credit card, including the cost of the medications. We had several credit cards with large limits, and I was used to making more than the minimum payments on the various credit cards to pay them off quickly. However, as the unsuccessful cycles mounted, we found ourselves overextended on credit and starting to show signs of financial distress.

I branded myself as a creative financer at some point. I told Angelique not to worry about the money aspect of things, and that I would find a way to make it happen, which I did. What that meant for me was taking a look at my 401(k) as a way to free up financial bandwidth. I decided to take out a 401(k) loan and create a debt consolidation loan, which consolidated several credit cards into one not low, but manageable, monthly payment.

I told myself that I was consolidating several of the early IVF/infertility cycles into a single loan that would be paid off in five years via a payroll deduction. I also told myself that I wouldn't feel the pain of that deduction because I was used to setting large amounts of money aside each month into my 401(k). At my peak I was setting aside $900 a month into this supplemental retirement account. The first of two IVF loans resulted in a $37,000+ loan and a $722.64 monthly payment back to me.

That was another thing I told myself: I was paying myself back. I was still young and could recover after it was paid off while still having an aggressive investment profile before dialing things back down to more conservative investments as I neared retirement.

What I didn't count on was not finding success with fertility treatments after doing that. Yes, it's true that I had freed up a few high-limit credit cards in case we needed more cycles, which we did. I didn't think we would need to switch IVF clinics, travel out of the area, or come out-of-pocket for new costs such as exploratory procedures or specialized bloodwork. I also didn't foresee us needing to pursue the surrogate route (which featured a surrogate coordination fee as well as legal fees) or the egg donor option (another egg donor fee plus an agency fee as well as legal fees). I told myself I didn't care what it cost to find success—we deserved to be successful.

So, I threw all of our financial might at what ended up being our last best chance—our sixth and final IVF cycle. That cycle was it: if we weren't successful, things were going to change in a major way. We were out of financing options, our savings had been depleted and Angelique was nearly forty, so taking another break wasn't necessarily a viable option depending on what we decided to do. Our last IVF cycle cost about $15,000 for the cycle alone. We found a wonderful donor, who was experienced and could command $10,000 for selling her eggs, but since we were splitting the haul with her, she only charged us $5,000.

We also had the agency fee associated with IVF cycle coordination, egg donor match and other administrative support. There were also some charges associated with the egg donor's expenses that were somewhat variable. God was looking out for us on that one, because thanks to her connections with the IVF and egg donor industry, she was able to keep our out-of-pocket costs to a bare minimum.

At one point I was compiling everything that needed to be paid for, and I was faced with the reality that we were a little short on the funds needed to make this magical cycle that featured the best of the best (best IVF doctor and best egg donor) possible. We didn't appear to have the money necessary to cover the egg donor's fee of $5,000.

I put on my creative financing thinking cap and analyzed what could be a source of the funding. I stumbled upon yet another retirement vehicle I had started early in my government career: my 457 deferred compensation plan. I could take out a maximum of two loans against each plan. I decided that I would take out a loan of $5,000 against my 457 plan and pay it back to myself over five years. The payment turned out to be $95 a month. I looked at that payment when I reviewed my paystub each month and I couldn't help but smile, as we now have three beautiful children as a result of that particular decision.

To make this final IVF cycle a reality, credit was utilized from a variety of sources. There was a slew of back and forth travel (flights for Angelique and/or me), fuel costs from driving, food and lodging, etc. And since we weren't working with a local clinic anymore, we were in unchartered territory and incurred new costs for remote monitoring. We went to third-party ultrasound and lab work clinics in Sacramento and had to pay higher fees since we were not doing any lab work through our Kaiser Permanente insurance provider's service offerings.

By the time we were done paying for all of these costs, I was getting credit card statements with extremely high minimum payments. We were both still working, so it was doable, but I knew it wasn't going to be sustainable if Angelique got pregnant and had a child. And I soon was greeted with a rather unpleasant confirmation of that reality.

We lost our home. The banks wouldn't work with us, despite our efforts. This was a very frustrating process. Looking only at the raw numbers, the banks would always conclude that I made too much money, and that there was no reason I couldn't keep making both mortgage payments.

When Angelique became pregnant with our triplets, she was on disability for over a year. This created new financial challenges. I was used to us both getting paid once a month. That's not the way disability payments work. There's a waiting period, so that meant that there was a loss of income for a specified period. And the Employment Development Department dispersed disability payments to claimants every two weeks.

This created challenges with paying bills and also making ends meet after the kids were born. The money received was less than her net pay, so that was a shortage each month for over a year after the children were born. And I made up the difference with what little savings we had left.

Eventually the disability payments stopped, and Angelique resigned from her state job. It was the right thing to do since the cost of childcare for triplets didn't make sense for our family. She worked so hard to have these children and she was just going to put them in daycare and essentially work for free? That simply didn't compute.

By the time the disability payments stopped, I knew things were about to get very ugly. I had never missed a payment on anything. My salary alone didn't cover everything, despite all of the adjustments I made over time such as eliminating cable, stopping pest control service, and reducing non-essential purchases.

Bold decisions had to be made. I consulted with contacts I had made over the years and gave them the highlights of our situation. Someone suggested an idea that I hadn't considered: filing for Chapter 7 bankruptcy. The difference between Chapter 7 and

Chapter 11 bankruptcy is that with Chapter 7, the debt is discharged, and you don't have to make back payments. Qualifying, given my high income, would be difficult, but the circumstances surrounding our financial hardship meant that there was a chance.

I sought the services of an attorney through my legal coverage with the state. This resulted in a $1,000 retainer fee for the attorney, but no out-of-pocket costs for me.

The early stages of preparing to file bankruptcy were tough. Both Angelique and I had to come to terms with the decision. It wasn't easy to stop making credit card payments. It wasn't easy at all to ignore the calls or to follow the script provided by the attorney (basically, the attorney told us to refer all inquiries to her office).

The whole experience was humiliating and humbling, but a necessary evil. We got the children we wanted. We didn't anticipate needing to incur more debt to buy things like diapers and large quantities of formula, but that's exactly what had to happen. We caught a break in other areas, though. We had a very successful fundraising campaign via GoFundMe, which funded many of the items the triplets would need over the course of their first year of life.

It took over two years after deciding to file for bankruptcy to actually file, because we had to wait for certain income to exit the six-month financial snapshot that was brought forward. That meant Angelique's disability payments needed to fall off. Then other events caused us to not pass the means test based on my income.

For example, I cashed out some of my vacation leave credits to help us stay afloat. That meant waiting another six months for that additional income to fall off of the snapshot. There were also concerns about the size of the tax refund we were receiving, thanks to the triplets. That money would be protected through the bankruptcy, although in two years we easily burned through both large refunds—triplets are expensive!

It was actually depressing filling out the bankruptcy profile. I had to identify all of the assets and liabilities. It was like taking a walk down memory lane—not only were our financial successes part of those memories, but so were all of the unsuccessful IVF cycles and dashed hopes and dreams. It was like watching it all circle the drain and be flushed away. There were no promotional opportunities at work, and there weren't many jobs being posted that aligned with my skillset.

It was a lot of stress. We both agreed that we didn't care about the house, so we pursued a short sale at the advice of our bankruptcy attorney. We found a rental in a really good area and moved in March of 2016.

I was very angry at the banks for not working with us. It didn't make any sense. It seemed as if we were being punished for making our payments on time and making good money. There were so many memories in that house, but we walked away from all of that. We chose not to play the games with the bank. I met with a realtor that specialized in short sales and he recommended that we stay in the house as long as possible and pocket up to $30,000 before being kicked out due to either foreclosure or the short sale going through.

There was no way I was willing to take that gamble. I didn't want to go out to lunch with the entire family and come home only to find that the locks on the house had been changed by the bank. I also knew our credit would be destroyed (which it was), and that would complicate acquiring a home to rent in a decent area.

Walking away, while humiliating, made the most sense. We cut our losses and didn't look back. The house sold fairly quickly via short sale. The first mortgage was made whole and the second mortgage company accepted a fraction of what they were owed. It was a horrible experience, but we survived it.

Only a handful of folks knew the extent of our financial struggles. I had learned to mask the pain of the various miscarriages we endured over the years, so I didn't let the financial stress show either.

Once the bankruptcy was filed, we felt partial relief. We had a case number, and there was a light at the end of the tunnel. It took nearly six weeks before the debt was officially discharged. Our financial situation had deteriorated to the point where I had to make installment payments of $85 a month on the bankruptcy filing fee.

I worked downtown and near the courthouse, so each month I walked or rode my bike to the federal courthouse. Those were very humbling walks and bike rides.

Eventually we had to meet with the trustee and answer a series of questions. Both Angelique and I were required to attend. I was handling everything related to the bankruptcy so that Angelique could focus on raising our children, so she had to come up to speed on the specifics. It was great that our bankruptcy attorney was there with us every step of the way. She told us what to expect question-wise, and we got to hear how others answered the questions asked by the trustee.

What was unnerving was when she told us that the creditors had the right to appear. I wondered if any of our creditors would show up to protest or question something. My relationship with our primary bank was all but destroyed. It was hard to go into the bank as everything was unfolding. I was advised to switch my direct deposit to a different credit union, which I did. My online access had been revoked. Paranoia set in. I was worried that if I used the ATM at that bank to pull out cash, that the ATM machine would "eat" my card. Any time I inquired about a loan I could still pay, like our car loan, I was reminded of the dire reality of our situation. It was so humiliating, but I had to continue forward.

When we received word that the debt had been successfully discharged, Angelique and I both felt that a huge weight had been lifted from our shoulders. Our infertility journey caused us to incur over $90,000 in additional debt over the course of seven and a half years. We were free to start fresh.

We would not be able to buy a home again for at least two years following the bankruptcy discharge. I have seen couples early in their IVF journey complain about potentially having to go into debt to have a baby. I immediately questioned how badly they want it. And even if it's not IVF, adoption is equally expensive and just as stressful.

I've come to the conclusion that giving up completely and having no kids would have been more costly to us both. That would have sent me into an unrecoverable debt with my wife. With the path we chose, she got three wonderful children out of it, and that makes it worth all of the sacrifice.

I hope that this chapter helps couples better understand the financial toll infertility can take on a marriage. Some people choose to not go into serious debt to have a child. Even with the bankruptcy behind us, things are still tight. The children have extraordinary needs, and it's not anything medical-related—it's food, clothing and other activities that support their development. And it's only going to get more expensive as they get older. But it was meant for Angelique and me to have triplets. We're the right parents for the job. Both of us grew up and watched our parents endure great sacrifices, and we're doing the same with our own kids.

So, if our teenage daughters ever tell us they hate us or that we don't love them at all, we will call absolute bullshit. We will tell them all that it took to bring them into this world, and remind them of the high cost of their precious lives and what we had to sacrifice. These children were an investment, of sorts. In a way they are a debt I'll never be able to fully repay. How do you repay three priceless miracles? The only thing I can think of is to give them the best upbringing I can and provide them with a ton of love.

We both went into debt for them. Angelique quit her comfortable job to devote her undivided attention to their development. We destroyed our collective credit. We willfully exited the role of homeowners. We both filed for Chapter 7 bankruptcy and God saw fit to allow me to pass the means test and for us to discharge the massive debt. We exhausted all of our savings accounts and currently live paycheck to paycheck. And we don't really complain about it, because there are many that are worse off. If that's not love, I don't know what is. Now, we live on a very tight budget. We hunt for deals, dress our kids in second-hand clothes and don't splurge like we used to. It's not about us anymore—it's all about them.

One day we'll be able to take a nice vacation with them. Eventually I'll be in a position to replenish all of the savings accounts and just maybe we'll be able to afford to enjoy our blessings. I've been working hard in my career to position myself to better provide for them. I went through the Leadership Academy for Information Technology, and eventually that substantial time investment will pay off.

To those couples looking into financing their attempt to have children, I hope that this chapter provides insights into everything that goes into that decision. The decision is a major one that could have unintended consequences. However, anything worth having requires tremendous sacrifice, this much I know.

Dear Dad

Dear Dad (William Bernard Cave),

When I was growing up as a child, you weren't around—you were at sea more often than not with the Navy serving our country. I never held that against you—you made the time you spent with us count.

It was a glorious feeling when you'd return and spend every waking moment with my sister Monissa and me. We'd do all kinds of things: visit the San Diego Zoo, picnic, go to San Diego Padre baseball games, and even visit the Toys R Us and PlayCo toy stores, despite Mom's advice not to (we always seized the opportunity to pit you and mom against one another).

When we'd learn you were going to be deployed again, it made us sad, and those first few hours after you'd say goodbye were pretty empty ones for me.

On April 7, 2008, you passed away. At that time, Angelique and I were very early in our journey to having children. Our mindset at the time was if it happened, great and if not, we had time. I didn't talk too much about our struggles with you because it hadn't yet become an obsession.

Diabetes took you from us, and the last time I saw you in person, your health had significantly deteriorated. You knew you didn't have much longer with us. In the years leading up to your death, I fielded many indirect questions from you about when we would give you grandchildren, but I didn't really know when, and clearly it wasn't up to me.

After you were gone, though, I'm sure you followed our struggle very closely, and I hope you are pleased with the outcome. These babies are a part of your legacy. I can only imagine what you would have thought after each pregnancy loss.

Something changed in me when you left us. The urge to have children of my own became stronger and stronger with each unsuccessful pregnancy attempt, so it would appear that I had a biological clock of my own. I tried my hardest not to put any pressure on Angelique, but the pressure was there anyway—how could it not be?

I guess part of it is me having a strong urge to leave my own legacy behind. It felt primal, and as the years went on, proved to be a difficult goal to accomplish. I poured my heart and soul into making it happen not just for me, but for Angelique as well. She sacrificed her body and mind to make this happen for our family. She was a zombie on autopilot for years before finding success. It was the only way she could continue on.

I remember when my sister Monissa gave birth to your granddaughter Christiana in 2003. You were so excited and were very involved in her life. You flew from San Diego, California and visited her in Norfolk, Virginia often and were a very positive influence in her life.

I remember conversations with you where you were talking about "Throwing in the towel" on the San Diego lifestyle. You talked about selling your condo in Lemon Grove, California and moving back East to be closer to family, specifically your other grandchildren based in the Washington, D.C., Maryland and Virginia region. You really lit up when you spoke of this vision. You spoke with conviction and were actively making plans to make it happen.

I can only imagine how much joy these beautiful babies would have brought you if you were still here with us—actually, I know you're watching from Heaven, and I know their arrival brought you great joy. I'm sure that you would have visited us immediately after the birth and stayed a while. I think you would have been proud that Christopher's middle name of William is your first name— you were one of the finest men I know, and an inspiration to me. Christopher would have loved hanging out in your lap and being the recipient of all of your goofy faces and tickles. He's already got a big personality that lights up the room, just like you. He looks exactly like me, and I look just like you, so if you looked into his eyes, you would melt—I just know it.

You were always good with babies and kids in general. I didn't particularly care much for kids growing up, but having your own changes you, and now it's a completely different feeling and experience for me. I am trying to be the best father I possibly can be for your grandkids. I didn't think twice about taking nearly four months off from work, because I didn't want to miss the special moments I got to experience.

It's extremely important for me to be there for them—it's no longer about Angelique or myself. I live to make and see them happy. There are so many deadbeat dads out there. To this day I can't see how you can bring a child into the world with another person and not be completely devoted to them. I know every situation is different, but it seems that, while sometimes it's for the best, willingly being absent in the child's life damages a child and leaves a lasting impact.

When we were a family before the divorce in 1989, you were trying to be the best father you could be. I didn't really know too much about you because you were away at sea, but I knew that I was loved, which was the most important thing. This is one of the reasons why I made it a point to come back to San Diego after graduating high school. It was extremely important for me to get to know you—after all, you are one of the reasons I am who I am today.

I wanted you to know that I really appreciate the latitude you gave me in college. You guided me but allowed me to develop in my own way and accumulate my own unique experiences. I put a lot of pressure on myself to make it through college, but you knew how to get me to see the big picture. I remember my second year of college, when I was taking a heavy unit load and we would only see each other on some weekends as a result, you got up one morning to make breakfast and asked me how my classes were going. I told you about a few of the tough classes and how frustrating it was, and you told me, "You know, son, C's get degrees. Last time I checked your GPA wasn't going to be printed on your college degree."

That made me smile and relax to the point where I knew how to better approach the rest of my college journey.

The reality of the situation is that I didn't really know *you* growing up. After you and Mom divorced, I still saw you doing everything you could to stay connected with us even though we were 3,000 miles apart. I received many letters from you, each addressed to "Master Michael Brian Cave". I thought that was awesome and a sign of respect.

Divorce can really wreak havoc on a child's development—depending on when it happens and the level of attachment, it can cause children to feel like they have to take sides. I never did that, though. To me you would always be Dad, and as far as I was concerned, whatever happened between you and Mom was between two adults, and there was no need for me to take it personally.

All that aside, I had a good childhood and can't complain. I just want what's best for our kids and I plan on being very involved. And this isn't because of you not being around when I was growing up (those are completely different circumstances). I want to be there because it's the right thing to do and I'm in the best position possible to make and keep that a priority.

We may not have had everything we wanted growing up, but we had all we needed. And even though you were at sea a lot when I was growing up, you made every effort to make each moment with us count when you returned home, no matter how short of a period that was.

Angelique and I have common goals when it comes to your grandkids. We want them to be individuals, not necessarily defined by being triplets. We want them to understand how they got here, and how much they mean to us. We also want them to understand what it means to be loved, and even though you're no longer with us, I know that you love them just as much as we do and are watching over them. Your presence is felt each and every day. There are subtle hints consistent with your legacy throughout the house. You *loved* dolphins. Go figure—Christopher tends to gravitate towards all things ocean, especially dolphins.

Rest assured that they will know who you were and what you represented to others. I want your grandchildren to be in a position to do what makes them happy. I want them to understand that all choices have consequences, and that they will have been given a solid foundation by the time they are ready to enter adulthood—that's what was done for me. Never, in my wildest dreams, did I think we would ever be parents of multiples, let alone triplets. I also didn't think it would take as long as it did, but looking back on our journey, it was worth the wait, as they are all gifts that keep on giving.

I think you would have been proud that Angelique and I didn't give up. We had a vision and did everything we could to make sure it became a reality. My drive I got from you, and I also learned to plan from you. You used to tell me

4 Thought = 7P:
Previous Proper Planning Prevents Piss Poor Performance.

I have never forgotten that. Once we graduated to IVF, those planning skills came in handy.

Knowing who you were when you were here makes it easy for me to imagine how you would have been with the babies. You would have spoiled them rotten. You probably would have joined Mom in acquiring custom license plates for your car to commemorate this triple blessing. While you would have certainly been retired and over seventy years old by now, you would have still had your friends at the horse wagering establishments and would have been sharing pictures of the triplets with them, and anyone else within a two-foot radius. You would have stopped by San Diego State University's bookstore and picked up three variations of the SDSU Grandad apparel, and would have demanded that they offer something for grandparents of multiples.

Let's not forget that no trip to San Diego would be complete without you dragging all of us to the casino. You would claim that certain people in the casinos were dying to see your grandkids, and while there we'd all be "bribed" with brunch or the buffet, and you'd place a few horse bets and sneak away to play Touch Easy Keno, with Christopher in your lap—oh my! You were always a good tour guide, yet I'm sure three babies clamoring for Grandad's attention would have forced you to figure out how to split your attention, but you would have figured it out, I'm sure.

When they were older and could appreciate a good meal, you would have certainly made your famous Navy breakfast of eggs, grits (yes - grits!), baked beans in bacon grease, and either white toast and jam or your famous (but not very good the next day) piping hot biscuits with jam.

Not only were you a great dad, but you were a phenomenal grandparent to each of your grandchildren. I know that they each brought you so much joy during your final years. It's true that I missed out on that, having not accomplished this while you were living, but things tend to happen in their own time, and everything happens for a reason.

Facebook has been a good way to keep both sides of the family informed. There are many family members, including a few of your other daughters, who are following this incredible journey from afar. So, the newest members of the Cave family have many admirers and are adored. I'm sure that your Facebook friends list would have been triple (no pun intended) the size of mine, given how well known you were. You probably would have taken on the role of evangelist for our cause at some point, too.

I remember when you had purchased a cruise for Angelique and me for our honeymoon, but we told you that we would rather have cash, as we were looking to move back to Sacramento and start a family. You handed us the check in advance of being married and said, "If you two don't go through with this, I want my money back."

You probably would have been perplexed with how much we ended up spending in order to be in a position to have these three blessings—over $90,000 over seven and a half years...crazy! You would have found a way to help out, I'm sure.

It's not that I hope you are proud of me—I know you're proud of me and the father I've become. But I hope also that you're proud of Angelique and me as a couple for sticking with this and not losing hope when it was so easy to just throw in the towel. We are pouring our hearts and souls into these precious babies. We've waited such a long time to experience parenthood and are taking full advantage of holding and kissing them all as much as we can before they start to assert their independence and not like that so much.

Parenting is a partnership. You were the breadwinner of the family, and Mom took care of the details, which included raising us. This also included the discipline. You had this look about you that commanded respect. You had a stern voice and a cold stare that oozed seriousness. I personally didn't want to ever discover the consequences of pissing you off. The thing is, you never laid a hand on me—ever.

When I was four, you were returning home from a tour at sea and I had been very bad that day. Mom told me to wait until you got home and I would be punished. She had everything ready—I called it mood lighting. There was a lamp in the room with a red-light bulb that really heightened anxiety, I must admit. However, when you got home, Mom told you how bad I'd been and that I was ready for you in the room and you told her you'd take care of it. You came in the room, gave me a hug and a kiss, and told me to go to bed. Maybe you were tired or something, or maybe you couldn't bring yourself to lay a hand on me. I certainly appreciated that gesture.

On another note, you wouldn't happen to know where Christopher got this exotic blonde hair from, would you? One of your other grandsons Lorenzo also has blond hair, so maybe it does run in the family? :)

Dear Mom

Dear Mom,

Thank you for all of your sacrifices while I was growing up. Thank you for supporting me through my life journey. You did a good job raising my sister Monissa and me, and this has helped me understand what it really takes to be a good parent. When you have children, (best case) your instincts kick in—this is why you hear people say, "Everything changed."

You raised me to be a good person. We were raised in a household with fair discipline, to have good manners, be independent and to set goals. We were also brought up to appreciate what we have—that's not working out so well with the triplets, as they destroy pretty much everything!

After you and Dad divorced, we struggled mightily at times, but this gave us insight into what it meant to make do with less and to find a way to survive. We didn't have everything we wanted, but we had all that we needed. And that's all that really matters at the end of the day.

You instilled things in me that I would need later in life. My future was always going to be based on a solid foundation as a result. I know it hurt when I left Norfolk, Virginia after high school to return to San Diego, but I had goals that I wanted to accomplish, and my gut told me that was the best move to make to achieve them. Regarding the solid foundation, I imagine that is why we were in Catholic school until high school. In private school, we were somewhat insulated from the harsher aspects of reality.

For example, I never saw a fight in school until I got to a public high school. And it was there that I first encountered youth with different priorities and no eye on the future. We had a comfortable life growing up in San Diego, and in the 80s, kids could be kids. We had basic rules that we had to follow, chores, and we were certainly not spoiled.

You are a twin yourself and are very close to your twin brother, Bernard. Never in a million years did I think that I would be a father of triplets, but I'm convinced now that things like this happen for a reason. Twins or even super twins such as triplets share a special bond that's hard to explain.

You invested a lot into your children. I find myself doing the exact same thing with our children, and I don't mean the financial investment. The creation of life is a tall order, and raising children is a difficult job—not everyone gets it right, that's for sure. I'm thankful that the triplets have given you so much joy these first few years. Technology has allowed you and others to stay connected to them in ways that would traditionally require frequent visits. Grandchildren are a blessing, and you were blessed with three new ones at once.

Your grandchildren are your legacy. You can see yourself in all of them—I know firsthand what an amazing feeling that is. I'm glad you got to meet them and get to know them. Children really are gifts from God. I know how much they mean to you, and don't worry, "Mima", they know exactly who you are.

Dear Angelique

Angelique, you endured great sacrifices to bring our three children, Michaela, Emma and Christopher into this world. For example, you endured that look from family or friends, wondering when you were going to have kids. You let some people in on your struggles, only to learn that they really didn't understand and couldn't relate. You've been bitter over this infertility struggle. You've been angry with yourself and I'm sure with me for putting you through this. You've endured incredible pain. You got comfortable with numbness as the losses mounted and ultimately became a zombie by the time we reached the last lap of the infertility race. You've probably fallen apart in the bathroom or shower more times than you'd ever admit to me.

I believe that everything happens for a reason, and I believe that we were destined to have not just three children, but triplets. I come back to your three cats, Blue, Nubay Cita and Cleo. In a way, it feels like God blessed you with three more children to love and cherish after you lost those cats. It also seems that in some way, each child has taken on specific aspects of each cat's personality.

For example, Blue was your first cat, and he was dominant around the other three. Michaela, our firstborn, is the same way, although in social situations she is completely the opposite. Nubay Cita kept to herself, much like Emma does, and loved to be held, just like Emma. She was also very whiny, just like Emma. Cleo often partnered with Blue to pester Nubay Cita, just like Christopher partners with Michaela to torment Emma.

When Dinky, the toy poodle, came into our lives, you tried to give him more love than he was comfortable with, having been on the streets for so long. Dinky was the perfect companion when you needed one the most, as we were on a break from trying to have children and were both uncomfortable with the void of not having a child. But you needed to love him, and you wanted him to love you back.

Infertility is a private issue that is often kept secret, and I know that it is something that you didn't expect to struggle with for so long. I know as the years went on, you thought about giving up, but you dug deep and found the will to carry on—this produced a truly incredible outcome.

We have three healthy and happy children who absolutely adore you, and while I know that they don't allow you to have a moment's peace, you are the reason they exist, and they need you. When you saw the three gestational sacs with strong heartbeats on the ultrasound monitor, you followed your heart and knew that you needed to keep all three pregnancies. You chose to give them each life, despite the risks. You didn't want to have to choose, as you did not feel you had any reason to have to choose.

I did not walk a single mile in your shoes. You endured so many painful needle injections, bruises and knots in your buttocks, unpredictable medication side effects, and had to be patient with your body until it was ready for you to try again. You sacrificed your immune system and wiped it out with antibiotics with each egg retrieval, and now, as a result, get sick with colds more easily. At one point, we thought that you could not carry a pregnancy at all, but you surpassed even your own expectations and carried triplets for twenty nine and a half weeks.

It was very hard for me to watch you beating yourself up over not being able to get pregnant on your own. There were many times where I couldn't find the words to say to try and make you feel better. I wished that I could protect you from all of the triggers that were present at the height of our struggles, but ultimately you did what you needed to do to protect yourself.

I know you were ashamed having seen so many others before you get pregnant so easily. I saw you at your lowest points over the course of this journey, but I also saw you put your own grief on hold and be strong for the both of us when I fell into a state of depression after we lost the twins in 2011. I saw how your spirt was lifted when you were confronted with compassionate care after we switched to Dr. Bradford Kolb's IVF clinic. Thanks to Dr. Kolb and his team, it was wonderful to see you have a positive outlook on our future after five previous unsuccessful IVF attempts.

"Job well done", or "Thank you" do not seem like the right words to express my appreciation for what you have accomplished for our family. You are incredibly strong, and your efforts to bring these beautiful children into the world has resulted in so many lives being touched.

By now you see just how special our children are. They leave a positive impression on anyone they come in contact with. You weathered the storm of depression, anger, despair and devastating miscarriages. You hopped back on the saddle again for our final IVF attempt, even though you had nothing left in the tank, emotionally. You had faith in others to carry you through portions of the race, but it was you who crossed the finish line.

These children of ours are our legacy. They wouldn't be here without your efforts—I'll never forget that. You love them each so much. They are your reward for your perseverance. After our fifth IVF miscarriage in January of 2014, I was certain that you were done. I could hear it in your voice when you'd talk about possibly trying again. You wondered what the point was, when it clearly wasn't working. You wondered why the outcome would be any different.

I didn't have any answer for you, but my persistent nature felt that it was worth asking you to give it one last chance by switching to the egg donor path. I hope you'll agree that this persistence paid off. After I asked you to try one last time, you probably asked yourself why this was so important to me. The answer is simple—you deserved to be successful. You were worth investing everything in. You were worth taking on even more debt. I happily bought plane tickets to whatever remote IVF clinic you needed to fly to in order to find success and happiness. You were worth taking on all of the administrative details of the IVF cycle so that you just had to focus on a handful of things. You were worth one final "high percentage shot" with our final IVF cycle using donor eggs. You deserved the opportunity to experience pregnancy and bringing a child into this world. You deserved a chance to make it farther in a pregnancy than you had previously, to walk those "next steps" that had been out of reach for so long.

You deserved a chance to shop at a baby department store for expecting mothers without feeling guilty for being in there. You deserved a chance to experience the nausea that comes with pregnancy. You had earned the right to don a pregnancy bump. And when the babies finally came, you had more than earned the right to decide that you wanted to quit working so that you could be a stay-at-home mom and have the full motherhood experience. Nobody gave it a second thought when you resigned from your comfortable job. You had waited seven and a half long years to be a mother, and you were not about to miss out on spending as much time as you could with the fruits of your labor.

Angelique, you should hold your head high. You are a very special person. You did what most people probably wouldn't do if they were in your situation, having endured so many losses—you kept going. When you were on bedrest at home and confined to that dark room with very little company throughout the day, I wondered what those days were like for you. There was so much uncertainty at that point in the pregnancy. You were tired of being confined to the room, but afraid to move around too much because the babies were so heavy. It couldn't have been easy for you knowing so much was at stake carrying triplets that could come at any day. We had no more money for any future attempts—this had to work.

I am extremely proud of your accomplishments, and I hope that you are too. You can take a deep breath and exhale, as you have accomplished an incredible feat. I know it's not easy to think of the early years of our infertility struggles, or to look at the photos we received of our embryos from our five previous IVF cycles, but it is clear that all of that happened for a reason. All of that prepared you for your current motherhood journey.

"Three things will last forever—faith, hope and love—and the greatest of these is love."

1 Corinthians 13:13

You, my dear, are love personified.

Dear Triplets

My Dearest Michaela Brielle Cave,

I predict that you will be a successful gifted public speaker, but first a model. Since you were born, your "owl eyes" have expressed a zest for life and an interest in people. You will grow up to appreciate diversity, which is essentially the differences in us all. You will light up the room most places you go, and your happiness will be contagious to others. You will end up being a vessel that brightens the days of those around you.

My words of wisdom to you are as follows: Always remember and appreciate the importance of family. You have a large one, and many people who love you so much. We hope by now you understand just how much your mother and I love you, and everything we did to bring you into this world and to be loved and appreciated. There's nothing that we wouldn't do for you three (within reason). We were blessed with the gifts that are you, your sister, Emma and your brother, Christopher. We trust that you will find meaningful ways to give back to others and influence lives in a positive manner.

We love you so much!

Love Always,
Daddy

Sweet Emma Grace Cave,

You could be a model as well, but I predict that you will be a counselor. You will use your intelligence to help others. People will be at ease when around you, as you have a very calming nature and a look that melts hearts. We could see it whenever anyone held you. The way you looked at each of us was always like you knew something that we didn't know. I looked forward to coming home to see you all after work. You will help others heal and/or realize their full potential.

At the time I wrote this, you had an easygoing personality, but I imagine you will continue to surprise us and to make us proud. You will master the art of making others happy and will have many opportunities to make friends. You are a beautiful young lady and will have many suitors. I'll make sure you and Michaela have reasonable standards. Regarding your career, I'm not guaranteeing you'll be a counselor, but just know that whatever you decide to do, I want you to be happy doing it and I will support your goals. Money isn't everything—be sure to make a difference. My words of wisdom to you are as follows: Trust your instincts and always be there for your siblings. You all will always have a special bond, and the three of you are a packaged deal.

Enjoy your future, Gracie :)

With All My Love,
Daddy

Dear Christopher William Cave,

You are our only son and were named after my older brother (Christopher is his middle name) and my father (William was his first name); these are two special men. You are a handsome young man by now, and you will be sought after by many women. It's a good thing we don't have a home telephone! I predict that you will be some type of scientist or engineer, as you love the outdoors and nature and love to build things. Who knows, maybe you will end up being an archaeologist and discovering long-lost ancient relics in Egypt. I just know that whatever you do, you will do it well.

You all mean so much to your mother and me. We can't even begin to attempt to put it into words. We waited seven-and-a-half-years to meet you three, and you've each brought so much joy to our lives, and we want to thank you for that. Realize that you've had a similar impact on others who have come in contact with you since you were born. There is just something so special about each of you. You remind us of how precious life is and humble us with your innocence.

I leave you with the following words of wisdom moving forward: Find a way to make a difference in the world. My father enjoyed making a difference in people's lives, whether it was in the Navy, with family or in the San Diego community. Protect your sisters—they are very beautiful young ladies and they'd do the same for you. Your mother and I will always be here for you. Continue to make us proud. Be respectful and humble, and don't forget to brush your teeth and floss each night, OK?

Love Always,
Dad

www.ingramcontent.com/pod-product-compliance
Lightning Source LLC
Chambersburg PA
CBHW030325080526
44584CB00012B/708